SECOND EDITION

DESIGNING ASSESSMENT
FOR MATHEMATICS

SECOND EDITION

DESIGNING ASSESSMENT FOR MATHEMATICS

EILEEN DEPKA

CORWIN PRESS
A SAGE Publications Company
Thousand Oaks, CA 91320

Copyright © 2007 by Corwin Press

For information:

Corwin Press
A Sage Publications Company
2455 Teller Road
Thousand Oaks, California 91320
www.corwinpress.com

Sage Publications Ltd.
1 Oliver's Yard
55 City Road
London EC1Y 1SP
United Kingdom

Sage Publications India Pvt. Ltd.
B 1/I 1 Mohan Cooperative
   Industrial Area
Mathura Road, New Delhi 110 044
India

Sage Publications Asia-Pacific Pte. Ltd.
33 Pekin Street #02-01
Far East Square
Singapore 048763

Printed in the United States of America

Library of Congress Cataloging-in-Publication Data

Depka, Eileen.
Designing assessment for mathematics / Eileen Depka. — [2nd ed.]
    p. cm.
Includes bibliographical references and index.
ISBN 978-1-4129-5274-3 (cloth : acid-free paper)
ISBN 978-1-4129-5275-0 (pbk. : acid-free paper)
   1. Mathematics—Study and teaching (Elementary)—Evaluation. 2. Mathematics—Study and teaching (Middle school)—Evaluation. I. Depka, Eileen. Designing rubrics for mathematics. II. Title.

QA135.6.D47 2007
372.7′044—dc22

2007002109

This book is printed on acid-free paper.

07   08   09   10   11   10 9 8 7 6 5 4 3 2 1

Acquisitions Editor:	Hudson Perigo
Editorial Assistant:	Cassandra Harris
Production Editor:	Veronica Stapleton
Copy Editor:	Cheryl Duksta
Typesetter:	C&M Digitals (P) Ltd.
Proofreader:	Tracy Marcynzsyn
Indexer:	Rick Hurd
Cover Designer:	Rose Storey
Graphic Designer:	Monique Hahn

Contents

Acknowledgments

Special thanks to the following people for their friendship, encouragement, and support:

Jeffrey Depka

Kay Burke

Barbara Zerwinski

Corwin Press would like to thank the following peer reviewers for the editorial insight and guidance:

Marcia Carlson
Sixth-Grade Teacher
Crestview Elementary School
Clive, IA

Beth Terry
Independent Consultant
Maine Math and Science Alliance
Brunswick, ME

Julie Duford
Fifth-Grade Teacher
Polson School District #23
Polson, MT

Gail Underwood
Second-Grade Teacher
Grant Elementary
Columbia, MO

Joy Wolfe
Fifth-Grade Teacher
Germantown, MD

Judith A. Rogers, EdD
Professional Learning Specialist
Tucson Unified School District
Tucson, AZ

Sherry D. Parrish, EdD
Elementary Mathematics
  Specialist
Hoover City Schools
Hoover, AL

Lee Ann Cervini
Principal
Holley Elementary School
Holley, NY

About the Author

Eileen Depka is a veteran educator and currently works as the supervisor of standards and assessment for the Waukesha School District in Wisconsin. While focusing on assessment, she works with teachers and administrators to organize and use data as part of the decision-making and goal-setting processes in an effort to increase student achievement. With the No Child Left Behind legislation as a constant focus, she helps administrators and teachers share data and implement practices to meet improvement goals.

A regular presenter at both local and national conferences, she is the author of *Designing Rubrics for Mathematics*, the *Applying Mathematical Concepts* manual, and the *Data Guidebook for Teachers and Leaders*, as well as articles on mathematics, assessment, and data analysis. Eileen has served as a content advisor for educational videos, a writer of online courses, and an instructor of graduate-level courses in education.

Driving all of her work is her passionate belief that all students can achieve high levels of proficiency and her dedication to educators in their quest to help all students experience academic success.

Introduction

THE STATE OF MATHEMATICS

In 1992, the National Assessment of Educational Progress (NAEP) presented a devastating report to the nation. More than 250,000 fourth-, eighth-, and twelfth-grade students in 10,000 schools nationwide were tested in mathematics proficiency. Although the results showed that the students had made significant gains in mathematics proficiency since a study two years prior, only 25% of students (and in some grades fewer) were deemed proficient in mathematics. One-third of the students tested did not even reach the lowest level of performance.

The NAEP published another report in 1996 stating that students at all grade levels showed an increase in scores on the 1996 test, which emphasized reasoning and communication within the mathematical standards identified as priorities by the National Council of Teachers of Mathematics (NCTM). The NAEP reported that 64% of fourth-grade students, 62% of eighth-grade students, and 69% of the twelfth-grade test takers were able to score at or above the basic level.

Although this report seemed to contain better findings than the 1992 report, the results showed that more than 30% of the students tested were not able to achieve even a basic level of performance, which means they were unable to achieve "partial mastery of prerequisite knowledge and skills that are fundamental for proficient work at each grade" (NAEP, 1998, p. 8). These results show that educators need to find instructional methods that are catalysts for breakthrough performance and in-depth mathematical understanding for all students.

In 2005, the assessment results showed 80% of the fourth-grade students were at or above the basic level of performance. Only 36% of those tested were at or above the proficient level. At the eighth-grade level, those numbers are 69% and 30%, respectively. Although these numbers reflect an increase over the previous year, as a nation, we have a long way to go.

In today's classroom, mathematics teachers need to teach mathematics differently from the way they were taught mathematics. The world has changed in many ways in recent years. The use and availability of computers and computer technology has multiplied, the Internet has become a common research and communication tool, and videos and video games have become popular. As a result, students have grown accustomed to various forms of brain stimulation and have come to welcome such forms of stimulation. Teachers lecturing while students take notes and complete routine problems from a textbook does not produce mathematics proficiency in all students. Students are not making the mathematical gains they deserve by working in isolation to complete worksheets or watching the teacher complete problems on the board; these practices do not reach all students (Black, 1994). As stated by O'Brien (1999), students need to be active thinkers and not simply memorize the thinking of others. Mathematics needs to make sense to students, and the best way for this to occur is through hands-on learning. Practices must change and new strategies must be employed to help today's students be successful in mathematics.

Many changes have occurred in the years following the 1996 NAEP study. Suggestions for new educational practices and techniques have flourished. Research shows that the classroom teacher and the strategies employed can and do affect the learner. New strategies (e.g., actively involving students through the use of performance tasks and problems that provide real-world applications) help students gain a deeper understanding of concepts and allow them to be better able to transfer that knowledge to new situations. Metacognitive methods and reflective writing are strategies that assist students in developing a new level of understanding because students learn to evaluate their thinking and the processes they use to arrive at solutions. Assessment results can be used to positively drive instruction, and gains in student achievement can be made when students take an active role in the learning process. However, to help students be successful, teachers must be willing to adjust, adapt, try new things, and teach in ways that they probably were not taught. Teachers need to step outside of their comfort zones to seek practices that will affect their students.

For educators, increasing student achievement must be a primary goal. Creating a nation of thinkers and active problem solvers who can use their skills in ways that demonstrate true understanding is crucial for student success outside the classroom. Relating schoolwork and textbooks to real-world situations helps students see a purpose for their education. Active engagement in the learning process helps students make the mathematical connections necessary for increased learning and understanding. Rubrics are a necessary tool for promoting student achievement because they provide students with a clear road map that shows how to achieve success by allowing learners to assess their work against criteria for various levels of performance.

ABOUT THIS BOOK

This book offers methods, techniques, and tasks that can be used to engage learners in the hands-on learning of mathematics. This book establishes the importance of using standards and benchmarks as educational targets to help students understand expected outcomes, and it stresses the importance of rubric development and the assessment process. The performance tasks actively engage the learners while allowing them to have fun in the process. Reflection opportunities provide students with the opportunity to evaluate their own performance and use that evaluation to grow and advance as math students. Data use is promoted to provide feedback to students and teachers about the strengths and challenges of students.

Each chapter concentrates on a different aspect of rubrics and the assessment process. Strategies and suggestions are based on the research and opinions of top educators and organizations.

The first section of every chapter lays the foundation for suggested practices. The second section, the "Rubric/Mathematics Application," suggests a performance task that relates to the information covered in the first section. A complete explanation of the application is provided, as well as the resources (e.g., task explanations, suggested procedures, rubrics, graphic organizers, charts, and assessments) necessary to implement the task in a classroom. An overview page (see Figure Intro.1) is included in each of these applications. This page encapsulates all the important information needed to carry out the performance task. The steps for each task are accompanied by thumbnail versions of the figures that make up the data charts, reflection pages, assessments, and rubrics for the task.

All of the performance tasks in this book are based on NCTM's *Principles and Standards for School Mathematics* (2000). Standards are the backbone of mathematics education and are currently the basis of almost all mathematics education programs in the United States. (More information regarding mathematics standards and their connection to rubrics is discussed in Chapter 2.) The various principles and standards each application focuses on are listed in the overview page. The mathematical application in each chapter is designed to allow students to demonstrate their level of understanding of the mathematics standards embedded in the application. Each application states a problem or task to be solved using mathematical skill, reasoning, and communication. The application also includes suggested procedures. These can be used to give direction to students who are not as familiar with performance tasks. (Performance tasks are opportunities for students to apply what they have learned in a real-life application.) For tasks with several steps or for more complex tasks, a task explanation and suggested procedures page are provided and can be handed out to students. Each chapter offers Internet resource links that can be used to promote technology research in the classroom, and figures are included in each application and can be copied for classroom use. Each application also contains information about time requirements. (Though activities in the book are based on 45-minute class periods, this time estimation may vary according to the level of the students, the use of calculators or computers, and the incorporation of task extensions.)

All of the mathematics applications in this book have been used with students and have produced outstanding results. Students who need to be challenged have found that the applications allowed them to grow and extend their capabilities, and students who find mathematics difficult have successfully completed the applications and developed a deeper

Rubric/Mathematics Applications Overview

Page Explanation

Standards:	Each project is linked to the NCTM Standards.
Mathematics concepts:	The concepts related to the performance are listed.
Grade level:	Suggested grade levels are stated, although they can be extended in both directions.
Related curricular areas:	Any curricular areas the project relates to in addition to mathematics are listed.
Materials:	This section lists any necessary supplies. It also states whether computers are needed.
Task:	The problem is a situation presented to students that sets the stage for a math connection related to the real world.
Suggested student procedures:	The procedures outline what students need to do to complete the task.
Teacher resources:	This is a list of the resource pages included in the chapter. The list indicates the pages that can be used with students.
Internet resources:	Each application includes several Web sites that are excellent resources for math teachers and students.

Figure Intro.1

understanding of mathematical concepts and their use. Extensions and simplifications are provided so each application can be differentiated for individual classrooms, students, and grade levels. In this way, low achievers, as well as gifted students, are able to achieve beneficial results. Expansions are also offered that help extend the performance tasks into other curricular areas, such as language arts, fine arts, and social studies. Such expansions are important as they incorporate an integrated, multiple-intelligences (Gardner, 1983) approach to learning. Technology is incorporated throughout the book in many ways—as a reference tool (to locate answers), as a construction tool (to build charts, graphs, or graphic organizers), and as a research tool (to find data).

Teachers can make a difference in the achievement of their students by providing them with experiences that have an impact on their learning and performance. Students who become engaged in learning through active involvement develop an in-depth understanding of mathematics, how it relates to them, and how it influences the world. The strategies and applications provided throughout this book can help teachers assist students in this process.

1

Using Rubrics in Mathematics

THE RUBRIC

According to *The New Merriam-Webster Dictionary* (Merriam-Webster, 1989), a rubric is a heading, title, class, or category. In education, however, it means so much more. A rubric is a scoring guide that can be used to make reliable judgments about a student's product or performance. It is a tool that distinguishes teaching and learning by clearly stating criteria and describing levels of quality.

According to Schmoker (1996), rubrics allow individuals to assess and track numerical data in an expanded way. Schmoker explained that rubrics can assess thinking skills, student understanding, and students' ability to apply their knowledge to mathematical tasks. The rubric gives teachers, students, and parents a reliable picture of what students should know and be able to do as well as to what extent they are able to demonstrate their knowledge. Schmoker also stated that a rubric—a set of written criteria used to analyze the outcomes of a student's learning—is "one of the most promising developments in assessment" (p. 70). Rubrics are based on educational standards and expectations and address not only what a student is expected to know and be able to do but also the level of quality he or she is expected to achieve.

According to Burke (2006), rubrics serve to assist students in improving their own performance. Rubrics provide students with the feedback necessary to set goals and demonstrate understanding at a higher level.

Rubrics are built on a rating scale. Scales vary, often ranging from 1 to 4, 0 to 3, or 1 to 6. The use of a specific scale is often a personal preference.

The scale of 1 to 4 is probably the most common because it is small, which helps keep students from being overwhelmed by descriptors, yet broad enough to encompass a wide range of quality descriptors. Typically, the scale of 0 to 3 is used when the rubric creator wants to use a 0 to represent no progress being made by a student toward a specific criterion. Larger scales, such as 1 to 6, are used when products are more involved and there is opportunity for a more widespread level of performance.

Rating scales contain concise descriptions for each level of progress. These criteria, or performance indicators, clearly state the level of performance expected at each numerical value on the rubric. The criteria stated within the rubric can help the assessor accurately evaluate students' work. Students too can use this tool to self-assess and improve their level of performance. The purpose of the rubric is not only to evaluate but also to help students increase their level of performance by outlining a vision of success.

There are two types of rubrics: analytic and holistic. The analytic format uses multiple descriptors for each criterion evaluated within the rubric (see Figure 1.1). In essence, a student's product has multiple opportunities to be evaluated within the same rubric. In an analytic rubric, "a performance is assessed several times, using the lens of a separate criterion each time" (McTighe & Wiggins, 1999, p. 273).

Example of Analytic Rubric

	1	2	3	4
Graph Title	Partially or inaccurately titled	Title unrelated to graph	Title related to graph	Title related to graph Perfect mechanics
Axes Title	Incomplete or illegible titles	Titles present but unrelated to axes data	Titles present and related to axes data	Titles present and related to axes data Perfect mechanics
X-axis Information	Incomplete or illegible information	Labels or numbers present partial inaccuracies	Labels or numbers present and accurate	Labels or numbers present, accurate, and easy to read
Y-axis Information	Incomplete or illegible information	Labels or numbers present partial inaccuracies	Labels or numbers present and accurate	Labels or numbers present, accurate, and easy to read
Key	Incomplete	Complete with inaccuracies	Complete and accurate	Complete, accurate, and easy-to-read
Graphed According to Key	No correspondence to key	Much graphed inaccurately	Graphed with minor error	Graphed according to key
Accuracy of Graph	Graph mostly inaccurate	Some inaccuracies	One inaccuracy	Graph completely accurate

Figure 1.1

A holistic rubric (see Figure 1.2) has one performance expectation description at each numerical level on the rubric. The product or performance is evaluated as a whole and often given a single score. The holistic rubric is, then, "a rubric used to obtain the overall impression of the quality of a performance or product" (McTighe & Wiggins, 1999, p. 277).

Analytic rubrics are best used as a part of the formative process. These rubrics are specifically designed as tools to improve student achievement through their use during any task or performance. Students are able to rely on the rubric descriptors to increase their level of performance. Holistic rubrics, in turn, are summative in nature. This type of rubric is most often used to evaluate work only at the end of a process. All rubrics used within this book are analytic rubrics, as these are the types of rubrics that best help to increase student performance.

WHY USE RUBRICS IN MATHEMATICS?

A myth surrounding the teaching of mathematics is thought to be true by too many: If the curriculum is covered, students will learn. Of course, all good mathematics teachers realize this is not the case, but often it is difficult for teachers to know what to do to better help students internalize the material. Teachers often wonder how students make mathematics their own and how they can help students personalize and make sense of mathematical concepts.

Student learning and understanding are often directly related to the variety of experiences within the mathematics classroom. According to Battista (1999), traditional methods in mathematics instruction fail to help students make connections to other situations where a mathematical formula might apply. Traditional methods have also proven to be ineffective as shown by the National Assessment of Educational Progress (NAEP) test results (see the introduction to this book). Students must be given numerous opportunities to form solid mathematical connections by solving real-world problems and making real-life applications.

In the traditional mathematics classroom, student work solely involves calculations. Answers are right or wrong, and, as a result, grading is fairly simplistic. These techniques, however, do not fulfill students' mathematical needs. National studies have shown that students from the United States are not competitive in mathematics worldwide. Studies such as those done by the NAEP have shown that a high percentage of students are unable to understand mathematics at a basic level. Adults in the United States often admit that they do not understand, and never will understand, mathematics. These indicators demonstrate that traditional mathematics methods may have done a good job of teaching calculations but a poor job of teaching thinking and application. Therefore, the focus in mathematics today has become one of active involvement, where students are able to calculate as well as think, apply, and explain their actions and processes. Cawelti (2004) indicated that students can achieve competence in procedures and calculations through the use of

Example of Holistic Rubric

ORAL PRESENTATION RUBRIC

Name: _____   Date: _____

Subject: _____   Final Grade: _____

5
The subject is addressed clearly.
Speech is loud enough and easy to understand.
Eye contact is good.
Visual aid is used effectively.
Presentation is well organized.

4
Subject is addressed adequately.
Speech has appropriate volume.
Eye contact is intermittent.
Visual aid helps presentations.
Organization is good.

3
Subject is addressed adequately.
Speech volume is erratic.
Student reads notes and has erratic eye contact.
Visual aid does not enhance speech.
Speech gets off track in places.

2
Speech needs more explanation.
Speech is difficult to understand at times.
Adequate eye contact is lacking.
Visual aid is poor.
Organization is lacking.

1
Speech does not address topic.
Speech cannot be heard.
Very little eye contact is made.
No visual aid is shown.
No organization is apparent.

Scale: 5 = A; 4 = B; 3 = C; 2 = D; 1 = Not Yet
General Comments:

Figure 1.2

Adapted from *How to Assess Authentic Learning* by Kay Burke © 1999 Corwin Press. Reprinted by permission of Corwin Press, Thousand Oaks, CA.

strategies that promote conceptual understanding and the construction of knowledge.

According to Bryant and Driscoll (1998), "Open-ended questions and other alternative assessments go further, which allows for richer responses from students and better data about students' mathematical content knowledge and problem solving skills. This information helps to inform teachers about where students are and what instruction they need to concentrate on. In order to be useful for the teacher, those data must be skillfully interpreted" (p. 27). Rubrics are the necessary tool for this type of skillful interpretation. Rubrics assess student outcomes and encourage student growth, enhanced performance, and increased levels of understanding. Through the use of clear, precise descriptors, student output can be categorized according to level of performance or understanding and a point value can be assigned to that level. Students can use rubrics prior to project completion to identify levels of quality and can use rubric descriptors to enhance their performance.

Increased use of a variety of performance tasks and analytic rubrics can be the key to increased student understanding and achievement because rubrics give students prior notice of the expectations for a given task or performance. Teachers should keep in mind that they need to share rubrics with students in advance of a task. Discussing the criteria with students is important so that rubrics do not become a top-down system like most assessments. If the indicators of success are not shared before the assignment begins, the rubric loses its effectiveness in aiding student success. Rubrics encourage quality by giving students access to clearly defined criteria and levels of performance. Rubrics also make students aware of the effort and accomplishment required to complete a task successfully. Through the use of various tasks and performances, students internalize mathematical concepts by engaging in the process of learning instead of simply memorizing the process used to reach an answer. Students see the relationship between a concept and its real-world applications and demonstrate a level of understanding far beyond a page of calculations.

Regarding the benefits of using rubrics, Schmoker (1996) stated that by clearly defining a performance, students see it as achievable. The rubric also provides students and parents with feedback that clearly identifies strengths and weaknesses—a characteristic that is not a strong point of traditional grading practices.

Rubrics help promote the goal of a sound education in mathematics, which includes developing "powerful mathematical thinking in students, [and] instruction [that] must focus on, guide, and support their personal construction of ideas. Such instruction encourages students to invent, test, and refine their own ideas" (Battista, 1999, p. 430). Rubrics are the evaluation tool necessary to aid in this task because they provide students with a guide to success and encourage them to reach for their goals.

The performances and tasks that encourage student success found throughout this book are called Rubric/Mathematics Applications. Each Rubric/Mathematics Application section outlines a mathematical task that puts rubrics into practice. The application for this chapter is titled "You're Right on Target!"

RUBRIC/MATHEMATICS APPLICATION

YOU'RE RIGHT ON TARGET!

This application was created to enhance skills in coordinate graphing. The application is based on three mathematics standards: geometry and spatial sense, communication, and problem solving. These standards, which are highlighted on the overview page, are addressed during completion of the task.

This Rubric/Mathematics Application is written at three levels of difficulty: primary, middle, and high school. Each figure provided is adapted to meet these three levels. These levels can also be used as a way to differentiate within a multilevel or multiability classroom. Students who need to be challenged can work at Level 3, students who are capable can work at Level 2, and students who need more foundational skills might function best at Level 1.

The application creates a problem for students to solve that requires the use of a variety of mathematical and communication skills. The problem may be presented to students with or without the suggested procedures listed within the overview. Students who are inexperienced in dealing with performance tasks or those who require more guidance will benefit from knowledge of the procedures. In classrooms where problem-based learning is commonplace, the task alone can be supplied.

For best results with mathematics applications, review all written information, teaching tools, and resources prior to presenting the task to students. Flexibility and creativity are encouraged, and throughout the unit suggestions are made to assist in restructuring this task to fit the needs of individual classroom populations and teachers.

The teacher resources within this chapter include instructions for the students and explanations for the teacher. All applications have answer keys. If teachers need additional resources or more information about coordinate graphing, the Internet is an excellent tool. A few Web sites are listed in the overview (see Figure 1.3) to get teachers started.

Performance Task Explanation

Students need to understand the meaning of coordinates and coordinate graphing before completing this task. During the completion of the task, students demonstrate an awareness and knowledge of graph numbering. During the task they locate the x- and y-axis and place stickers at the intersections of lines on the graph paper. Then, they accurately identify the coordinates at which the stickers are placed. This task takes about two to four 45-minute class periods depending on the use of expansion activities.

The task is designed with three levels of difficulty. Younger students use large grid paper and 12 stickers. They use six stickers to identify coordinates and six stickers on their Student Answer Record Charts. Students in the middle grades place 30 stickers on more detailed graph paper and list 20 coordinates. Students in the upper grades use four-quadrant graph paper and place 30 stickers on the paper, making certain that at least 6 stickers are placed in each quadrant. Students in every level identify the coordinates of all the stickers. The activity may be done as a class, in cooperative groups, or independently.

Unit Overview

You're Right On Target!

Standards:	Geometry and Spatial Sense, Communication, Problem Solving
Mathematics concepts:	Coordinate graphing
Grade levels:	2 through 10
Related curricular areas:	Social studies—map skills; language arts—writing directions; art—design packaging
Materials:	Assorted stickers, grid paper (blackline master included)
Task:	Quadrant Brothers Toy Company is in the process of creating a new strategy game. The game consists of locating hidden targets on a graph by guessing the location's coordinates. Players are given hints relating to the location of the hidden targets. The game contains hundreds of different graphs. The company needs your help to create the graphs and target locations as well as to provide answer keys for the players.

Suggested Student Procedures

1. Choose stickers and place them at various intersections on a grid (piece of graph paper).
2. Label and number the x-axis (horizontal axis).
3. Label and number the y-axis (vertical axis).
4. Create a title for the graph.
5. Create an answer key for the graph that lists the coordinates of the stickers. Place the coordinates on the chart provided.

Teacher Resources

Student Task Sheet for three levels

Student Answer Record Chart for three levels

Rubric for three levels

Graph checklist for all levels

Checkup and key for three levels

Reflections for all levels

Internet Resources

Math Matters: Contains information on combating mathematics anxiety, such as information on brain research and metalearning, as well as tips and strategies on helping students feel more comfortable with mathematics. (http://www.mathmatters.net/matips.htm)

Quick Math Site: Provides help to mathematics questions in various areas, including graphing. (for higher levels; www.quickmath.com)

Figure 1.3

Figure 1.4　　　**Figure 1.5**　　　**Figure 1.6**

Figure 1.7　　　**Figure 1.8**　　　**Figure 1.9**

Figures 1.4 to 1.6 contain task sheets for all three levels, and Figures 1.7 to 1.9 contain the record charts for all three levels. To complete the activity, students should be given copies of the Student Task Sheet and record chart. The record chart serves as a graphic organizer to help students organize their data and list the coordinates. Students may want to create their own graphic organizer to house the information, and teachers should encourage this.

Teachers should make stickers available for the students. Large stickers may work better with younger students, and ministickers or dots may work better with older

Figure 1.10　　　**Figure 1.11**　　　**Figure 1.12**　　　**Figure 1.13**

students who are using smaller spaced graph paper. A time limit for choosing stickers can be given to students in advance to keep the task focused.

Rubric

Students should be aware of task expectations before beginning. Give each student or cooperative group a copy of the rubric, which is based on a 0 to 3 scale, at the start of the activity. Take a few minutes to highlight the expectations for the performance task. This will result in higher quality products. The 3-point section on the rubric should be clear to the students so they understand how to aim for the highest level of achievement. Rubrics for each level are offered in Figures 1.10 to 1.12.

Checklist

Students may begin the task after viewing the rubric. As students complete their graphs, the checklist (see Figure 1.13) of components to be demonstrated in the completed work provides reminders relating to all of the graph components.

Students should be given the opportunity to self-assess or peer-assess before their work is turned in. The self-reflection prompted by rubric scoring results in students reaching for a higher level of quality. Students should be given a chance to enhance their performance by meeting high-level rubric descriptors. As students get used to using rubrics, they become very good at evaluating their peers and helping one another. Sometimes students do not realize that they are missing a component and are pleased when a peer points it out to them. This practice helps improve student performance and elevates students' level of achievement.

Peers and parents also can be encouraged to complete a rubric for task evaluation. Peer and parent reactions are especially beneficial when the rubric is used as a tool to assist students before the task is graded. Students can use parent and peer input to affirm, improve, and expand their product as necessary or appropriate.

Finally, the product should be submitted for teacher evaluation. When grading the finished products, teachers can circle or highlight the numerical rubric value most appropriate to the level of student performance. When rubrics are complete and a grade needs to be determined, the rubric score can be used as a grade, or it can be converted into a percent by dividing the total points earned by the total points possible. The grading scale will vary depending on individual grading scales and scoring practices.

Expanding the Task

To extend this performance task into the area of language arts, ask students to write step-by-step directions for the game. Directions should include ways the game might best be organized and played. Emphasize creativity and clear communication skills. Students can also create game rules and strategies.

To extend this task into the art classroom, students can use their artistic skills to design packaging for the game, such as a game logo or a decorative cover. A large manila envelope can be used as a container for the game.

Simplifying the Task

The performance task is fairly simple and can be easily completed in one class period. However, if further simplification is needed, the task can be accomplished as a

Figure 1.14

Figure 1.15

Figure 1.16

Figure 1.17

Figure 1.18

Figure 1.19

Figure 1.20

Figure 1.21

large- or small-group activity instead of independently. Another way to simplify is to ask students to identify fewer coordinates.

Playing the Game

Students can use their graphs to actually play the game. Each graph creator should be paired up with a classmate who guesses the coordinate location of a sticker. The graph creator tells the guesser if he or she is right or wrong. If the guesser is wrong, the creator gives the guesser a hint by telling him or her the direction to go in to get to the closest sticker. For example, the creator might tell the guesser that the closest sticker is to the southwest, or he or she might tell the guesser that the sticker is someplace west of 3 and north of 5. Guessers should keep track of their guesses to make plans for future responses. Guessers need a blank piece of graph paper to do this.

The game can be played as an entire class with younger students. Using large graph paper, one side of the room can become the creators and the other side the guessers. Roles can be switched after the first game is complete.

Checkup

The checkup for each level is shown in Figures 1.14 to 1.16. These checkups are teacher-made assessments that can be used as practice tasks or tests. Students are asked to identify the coordinates of points on a grid. The task is designed at three levels of difficulty. Using the task before the game reveals whether students have the skills necessary to complete the activity. Using it as a postactivity assessment determines whether students understand coordinates and their relationship to a fixed position on a graph. Answer keys to the tests are provided in Figures 1.17 to 1.19.

Mathematics Reflection

The Mathematics Reflection page (see Figure 1.20) can be used as a brief follow-up activity. The page asks students what they learned and what they liked about the task they just completed. The reflection is a form of metacognition, or thinking about thinking, and is similar to a journal entry.

Metacognition is a valuable tool because it helps students clearly articulate what they have learned as well as understand their strengths and weaknesses. Through the process of metacognition, students are challenged to understand their own thought processes and, as a result, are more likely to transfer their learning to other situations. A completed reflection page is provided in Figure 1.21 as an example of how students might reflect on this task.

IN SUMMARY

The rubric is the tool that binds assessment and student achievement by making students and parents aware of expectations from the onset. When this occurs, achievement at a high level of performance is a natural outcome. There are no surprises for students during the evaluation process with the rubric.

Rubrics also make grading easier and less messy for teachers. Evaluation is not only about whether the answer is right or wrong, but it is also about critiquing the steps used along the way. Rubrics provide teachers with clear guidelines to make the grading process less subjective and more concrete.

You're Right On Target!

Student Task Sheet   **Level 1**

1. Choose a total of twelve stickers, two of each kind.
2. Place one of each kind at different locations on the grid. Make sure that the stickers are placed where lines meet.

   Like this   or this

3. Number the x-axis and the y-axis.
4. Create a title for the graph.
5. Place one of each sticker in the sticker column on the Student Record Chart. Write the coordinates for each sticker placed on the graph. (Remember that the number on the x-axis comes first.)

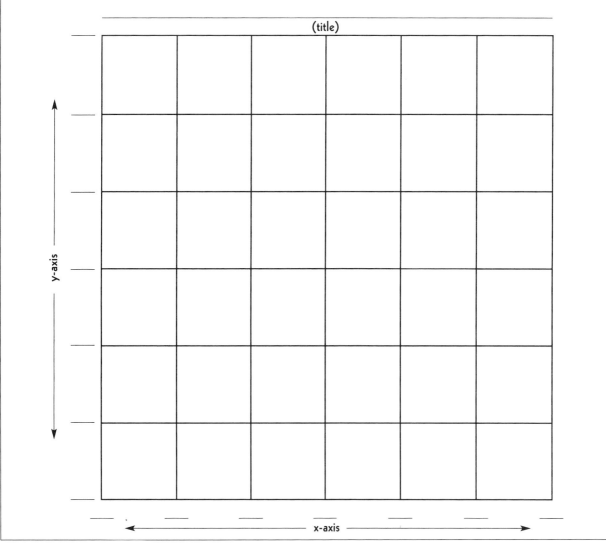

Figure 1.4

You're Right On Target!

Student Task Sheet   **Level 2**

1. Choose 20 stickers. Carefully place them at different locations on the grid, making sure you put the stickers at line intersections. Number each sticker so it can be easily identified.
2. Number the *x*-axis and the *y*-axis.
3. Create a title for the graph.
4. Fill in the Student Record Chart. Write the identification number and the coordinates for each sticker placed on the graph.

(title)

Figure 1.5

You're Right On Target!

Student Task Sheet   **Level 3**

1. Choose 30 stickers. Carefully place them at different locations on the grid making sure to put the stickers at line intersections. Number each sticker so it can be easily identified. Place at least six stickers in each quadrant.
2. Number the *x*-axis and the *y*-axis.
3. Create a title for the graph.
4. Fill in the Student Record Chart. Write the identification number and the coordinates for each sticker placed on the graph.

(title)

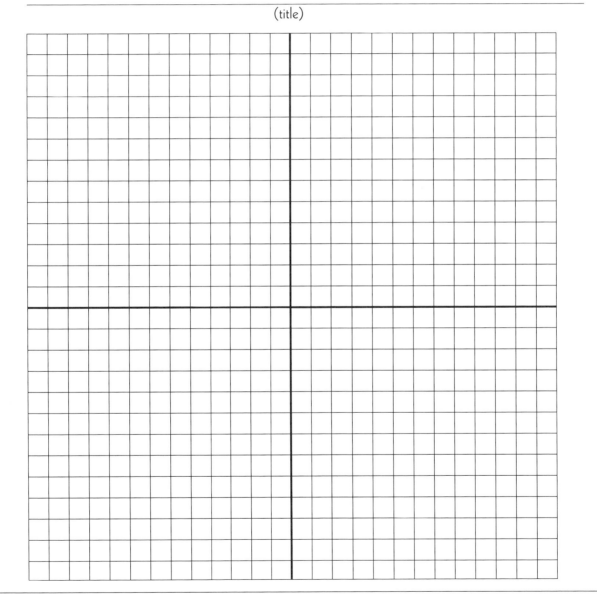

Figure 1.6

You're Right On Target!

Student Record Chart   Level 1

1. Place one of each type of sticker in the sticker column.

2. Write the coordinates for each sticker in the second column.

Sticker	Coordinates (x, y)

Figure 1.7

You're Right On Target!

Student Record Chart   Level 2

1. Write the sticker identification number in the first column.

2. Write the coordinates for each sticker in the second column.

Sticker Identification Number	Coordinates (x, y)

Figure 1.8

You're Right On Target!

Student Answer Record Chart　　　　　　　　　　　Level 3

1. Write the sticker identification number in the sticker column.

2. Write the coordinates for each sticker in the coordinates column.

Sticker Identification Number	**Coordinates** (x, y)	**Sticker** Identification Number	**Coordinates** (x, y)

Figure 1.9

You're Right On Target!

Rubric
Level 1

Instructions: Choose the point value that best describes the performance in each category.

	0 *You missed!*	1 *You're on the edge!*	2 *You're getting closer!*	3 *You're right on target!*	*Points Earned*
Graph Numbering x-axis	Not present or inaccurate	Complete	Complete, accurate	Complete, accurate, neat	
y-axis	Not present or inaccurate	Complete	Complete, accurate	Complete, accurate, neat	
Graph Title	Not present or inaccurate	Present with spelling and capitalization errors	Present with spelling or capitalization errors	Present with accurate spelling and capitalization	
Sticker Placement	Inaccurate placement of all stickers	1 or 2 stickers accurately placed on grid	3 to 5 stickers accurately placed on grid	All stickers accurately placed on grid	
Coordinates #1	Inaccurate	Accurate coordinates, missing comma and parentheses	Accurate coordinates, missing comma or parentheses	Accurate coordinates, including comma and parentheses	
#2	Inaccurate	Accurate coordinates, missing comma and parentheses	Accurate coordinates, missing comma or parentheses	Accurate coordinates, including comma and parentheses	
#3	Inaccurate	Accurate coordinates, missing comma and parentheses	Accurate coordinates, missing comma or parentheses	Accurate coordinates, including comma and parentheses	
#4	Inaccurate	Accurate coordinates, missing comma and parentheses	Accurate coordinates, missing comma or parentheses	Accurate coordinates, including comma and parentheses	
#5	Inaccurate	Accurate coordinates, missing comma and parentheses	Accurate coordinates, missing comma or parentheses	Accurate coordinates, including comma and parentheses	
#6	Inaccurate	Accurate coordinates, missing comma and parentheses	Accurate coordinates, missing comma or parentheses	Accurate coordinates, including comma and parentheses	

Points possible = 30

Evaluator: _____   Points earned = _____

Figure 1.10

You're Right On Target!

Level 2

Rubric

Instructions: Choose the point value that best describes the performance in each category.

	0 *You missed!*	1 *You're on the edge!*	2 *You're getting closer!*	3 *You're right on target!*	*Points Earned*
Graph Numbering x-axis	Not present or inaccurate	Complete	Complete, accurate	Complete, accurate, neat	_____
y-axis	Not present or inaccurate	Complete	Complete, accurate	Complete, accurate, neat	_____
Graph Title	Not present or inaccurate	Present with spelling and capitalization errors	Present with spelling or capitalization errors	Present with accurate spelling and capitalization	_____
Sticker Placement	Inaccurate placement of all stickers	1 to 2 stickers accurately placed on grid	3 to 5 stickers accurately placed on grid	All stickers accurately placed on grid	_____
Coordinates #1–4	Inaccurate	1 accurate pair of coordinates, including comma and parentheses	2 to 3 accurate pairs of coordinates, including comma and parentheses	All accurate coordinates, including comma and parentheses	_____
#5–8	Inaccurate	1 accurate pair of coordinates, including comma and parentheses	2 to 3 accurate pairs of coordinates, including comma and parentheses	All accurate coordinates, including comma and parentheses	_____
#9–12	Inaccurate	1 accurate pair of coordinates, including comma and parentheses	2 to 3 accurate pairs of coordinates, including comma and parentheses	All accurate coordinates, including comma and parentheses	_____
#13–16	Inaccurate	1 accurate pair of coordinates, including comma and parentheses	2 to 3 accurate pairs of coordinates, including comma and parentheses	All accurate coordinates, including comma and parentheses	_____
#17–20	Inaccurate	1 accurate pair of coordinates, including comma and parentheses	2 to 3 accurate pairs of coordinates, including comma and parentheses	All accurate coordinates, including comma and parentheses	_____
Neatness	Sloppy, difficult to read	Can be read with careful concentration	Neat, some room for improvement	Perfectly neat!	_____

Evaluator: _____   Points possible = 30   Points earned = _____

Figure 1.11

You're Right On Target!

Rubric   Level 3

Instructions: Choose the point value that best describes the performance in each category.

	0 *You missed!*	**1** *You're on the edge!*	**2** *You're getting closer!*	**3** *You're right on target!*	*Points Earned*
Graph Numbering x-axis	Not present or inaccurate	Complete	Complete, accurate	Complete, accurate, neat	___
y-axis	Not present or inaccurate	Complete	Complete, accurate	Complete, accurate, neat	___
Graph Title	Not present or inaccurate	Present with spelling and capitalization errors	Present with spelling or capitalization errors	Present with accurate spelling and capitalization	___
Sticker Placement	Inaccurate placement of all stickers	1 to 2 stickers accurately placed on grid	3 to 5 stickers accurately placed on grid	All stickers accurately placed on grid	___
Coordinates #1–6	Inaccurate	1 accurate pair of coordinates, including comma and parentheses	2 to 3 accurate pairs of coordinates, including comma and parentheses	All accurate coordinates, including comma and parentheses	___
#7–12	Inaccurate	1 accurate pair of coordinates, including comma and parentheses	2 to 3 accurate pairs of coordinates, including comma and parentheses	All accurate coordinates, including comma and parentheses	___
#13–18	Inaccurate	1 accurate pair of coordinates, including comma and parentheses	2 to 3 accurate pairs of coordinates, including comma and parentheses	All accurate coordinates, including comma and parentheses	___
#19–24	Inaccurate	1 accurate pair of coordinates, including comma and parentheses	2 to 3 accurate pairs of coordinates, including comma and parentheses	All accurate coordinates, including comma and parentheses	___
#25–30	Inaccurate	1 accurate pair of coordinates, including comma and parentheses	2 to 3 accurate pairs of coordinates, including comma and parentheses	All accurate coordinates, including comma and parentheses	___
Neatness	Sloppy, difficult to read	Can be read with careful concentration	Neat, some room for improvement	Perfectly neat!	___

Evaluator: _____   Points possible = 30   Points earned = ___

Figure 1.12

You're Right On Target!

Graph Checklist   **All Levels**

Place an X in the box that best describes the work you have completed on your graph.

	Yes!	I'm still working on it.
Graph has a title.		
Title is capitalized appropriately.		
Title relates to graph.		
x-axis is numbered.		
Numbers are neat.		
y-axis is numbered.		
Numbers are neat.		
All stickers are placed at various line intersections.		
All coordinates are complete.		
x-axis number is the first coordinate.		
Coordinates are in parentheses.		
A comma is between coordinates.		

Figure 1.13

You're Right On Target!

Checkup   Level 1

On the chart below, list the coordinates for all of the creatures.

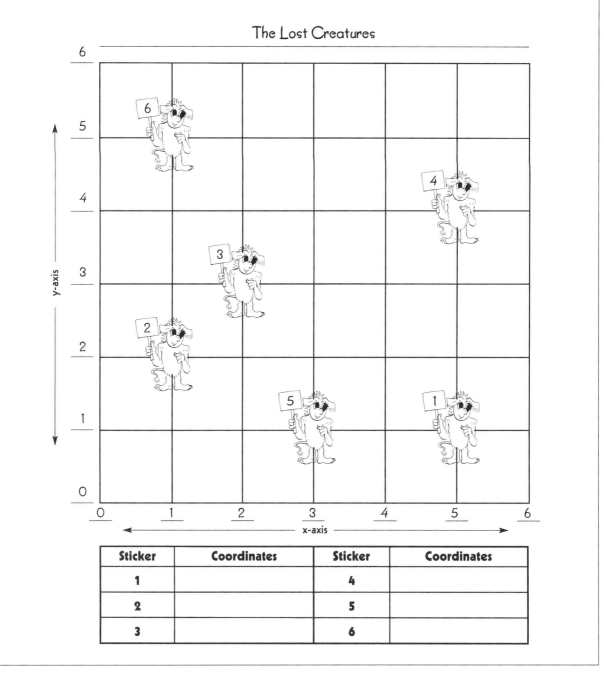

Sticker	Coordinates	Sticker	Coordinates
1		4	
2		5	
3		6	

Figure 1.14

You're Right On Target!

Checkup   Level 2

List the coordinates of each teddy bear on the chart below the graph.

#	Coordinate	#	Coordinate	#	Coordinate	#	Coordinate
1		6		11		16	
2		7		12		17	
3		8		13		18	
4		9		14		19	
5		10		15		20	

Figure 1.15

You're Right On Target!

Checkup   **Level 3**

List the coordinates of each soccer ball on the chart below the graph.

#	Coordinate	#	Coordinate	#	Coordinate	#	Coordinate
1		6		11		16	
2		7		12		17	
3		8		13		18	
4		9		14		19	
5		10		15		20	

Figure 1.16

You're Right On Target!

Checkup – Key   Level 1

On the chart below, list the coordinates for all of the creatures.

Sticker	Coordinates	Sticker	Coordinates
1	(5,1)	4	(5,4)
2	(1,2)	5	(3,1)
3	(2,3)	6	(1,5)

Figure 1.17

You're Right On Target!

Checkup – Key   **Level 2**

List the coordinates of each teddy bear on the chart below the graph.

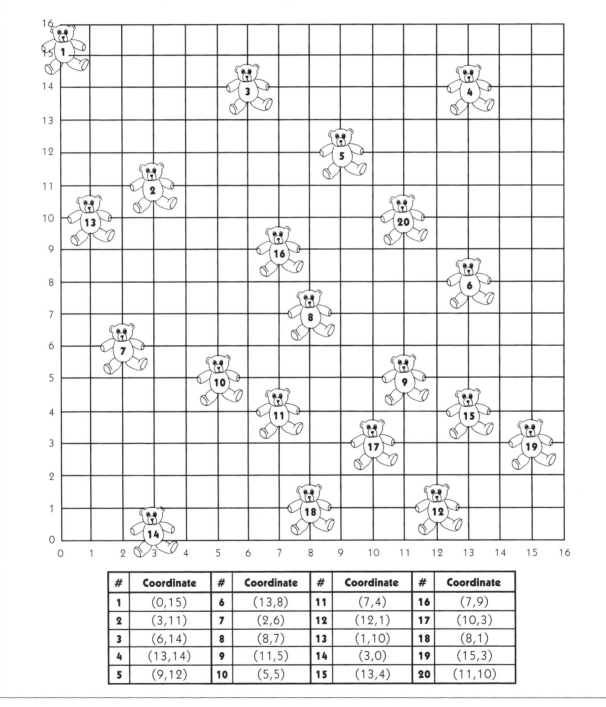

#	Coordinate	#	Coordinate	#	Coordinate	#	Coordinate
1	(0,15)	6	(13,8)	11	(7,4)	16	(7,9)
2	(3,11)	7	(2,6)	12	(12,1)	17	(10,3)
3	(6,14)	8	(8,7)	13	(1,10)	18	(8,1)
4	(13,14)	9	(11,5)	14	(3,0)	19	(15,3)
5	(9,12)	10	(5,5)	15	(13,4)	20	(11,10)

Figure 1.18

You're Right On Target!

Checkup – Key **Level 3**

List the coordinates of each soccer ball on the chart below the graph.

#	Coordinate	#	Coordinate	#	Coordinate	#	Coordinate
1	(8,7)	6	(-1,2)	11	(-9,-1)	16	(3,-4)
2	(5,2)	7	(-4,5)	12	(-1,-2)	17	(6,-7)
3	(11,4)	8	(-12,11)	13	(-1,-9)	18	(0,-5)
4	(3,10)	9	(-2,5)	14	(-11,-9)	19	(11,-12)
5	(0,7)	10	(-5,2)	15	(-5,-6)	20	(13,-2)

Figure 1.19

You're Right On Target!

Reflections   **All Levels**

In the space provided, write your reflections on the graphing task.

I learned: _____
_____
_____
_____
_____
_____
_____
_____
_____
_____
_____

I liked: _____
_____
_____
_____
_____
_____
_____
_____
_____
_____
_____

Figure 1.20

You're Right On Target!

Reflections   **All Levels**

In the space provided, write your reflections on the graphing task.

I learned: _____

    Lots of things about coordinate graphing and labeling graphs. I know

       how to place points without mistakes.

_____

_____

_____

_____

_____

_____

_____

_____

I liked: _____

    The game. It was fun to have someone guess where my stickers

    were. I had fun guessing, too. I can remember coordinates

    better now. I know the x comes before the y and x is on the

    horizontal axis.

_____

_____

_____

_____

_____

_____

Figure 1.21

The Relationship Between Mathematics Standards and Rubrics

THE IMPORTANCE OF STANDARDS

When a house is built, a strong foundation is of utmost importance. Without it, the structure is unstable, unpredictable, and perhaps even unsafe. In education, standards form the foundational framework. They keep the structure solid and dependable. Standards guarantee students that their education is built on firm ground and is consistent with the education being received by others.

Standards are the educational guidelines for instruction and provide educators with the broad expectations students should achieve. Standards are broad categories of knowledge that experts deem essential to learning in specific fields of study. In the *Principles and Standards for School Mathematics* (2000), the National Council of Teachers of Mathematics (NCTM) identified 10 standards—5 content and 5 process. The five content standards include numbers and operations, algebra, geometry, measurement, and data analysis and probability. The process standards include problem solving, reasoning and proof, communication, connections, and representation. Identifying and using standards is crucial to teaching mathematics throughout the United States because standards provide a mathematical focus for instruction. Ideally, with the widespread use of standards, all students throughout the country are guaranteed the same mathematical concept focus. Currently, 49 states have adopted standards for their educational systems.

According to Fitzpatrick (1998), a coherent vision of student learning is necessary for a program of study to maintain focus. With standards as the focus, the foundation needed to create learning experiences that promote excellence in education and affect student performance is in place.

Benchmarks go hand in hand with standards. Benchmarks are more specific and indicate performance expectations for every student. Benchmarks are expectations that describe what students should know and be able to do within each standard. For example, according to the NCTM (2000), a geometry standard at the third- and fifth-grade level states that students should "apply transformations and use symmetry to analyze mathematical situations" (p. 164). A more specific expectation or benchmark indicates that students should "predict and describe the results of sliding, flipping, and turning two-dimensional shapes" (p. 164).

Together, standards and benchmarks create the vision of lesson outcomes. They let educators know in advance the essential knowledge required for a lesson to be considered successful. Standards and benchmarks help increase student performance because they indicate the expectations for all students. Student performance and achievement are compared to standards and benchmarks, and that comparison can then be used as a measurement of success. With standards and benchmarks, high expectations are present for all students and all are expected to achieve. When there is a genuine commitment to standards-based achievement, comparing students to the average becomes truly unnecessary (Reeves, 1998). Students in a standards-based classroom are not compared to other students to determine their standing in the class or their grade on a performance because the standards provide the basis for comparison.

The goal of standards-based education is for all students to be winners and perform to their highest potential. All students are aware of the standards they need to reach; the educator's job is to assist them on their road to achievement. State and district standards and benchmarks clearly define expectations; educators provide experiences that assist students in understanding concepts and constructing meaning according to the expectations outlined within the standards and benchmarks (Zemelman, Daniels, & Hyde, 1993). Teachers can provide such experiences by using performance tasks and providing real-life experiences for their students. These types of tasks are discussed further in Chapter 3.

MATHEMATICS STANDARDS AND RUBRICS

According to the NCTM, standards are a prototype that can be viewed as a professional consensus of what is deemed important to the understanding of mathematics (Crosswhite, Dossey, & Frye, 1989). The standards are a compilation of what educators have endorsed as the practices and concepts necessary to create a sound mathematics program. The NCTM standards provide guidance for daily classroom experiences, and most schools use standards that are based on those compiled by the NCTM. The NCTM publication *Principles and Standards for School Mathematics* (2000) contains five standards that reflect crucial mathematical content and an additional five process standards that emphasize mathematical learning and understanding. Process standards aim to ensure that students can go beyond computation into mathematical interpretation, problem solving, and communication to develop a deep understanding of mathematical concepts. The NCTM standards are used as the basis for all mathematics units within this book, and they are also the mathematics standards used by educational systems throughout the United States. Although schools or districts may present their mathematics standards in a different format from the NCTM standards, the concepts are the same as those found in the NCTM. For more information on the NCTM standards, visit the NCTM Web site at www.nctm.org.

Using the district or state standards and benchmarks for the grade level as a guide, teachers must determine the specific skills and essential knowledge to be learned prior to developing an instructional plan. Burke (2006) stated that "the standards dictate the performance students need to be able to demonstrate" (p. 78). Identifying the standards and benchmarks helps to successfully develop a quality task. Teachers can use rubrics as an organizational tool to display criteria and show explicit expectations for a quality performance. Rubrics allow teachers to organize the benchmarks into a format that students can use as guidelines in a learning application. Whereas standards establish the focus of the learning, the rubric provides the evaluation tool.

Creating a Rubric That Addresses Standards

When developing a rubric, it is important for teachers to keep in mind a picture of exemplary student performance and consider the following questions among others:

- What will success look like?
- What are the expected levels of quality?
- How will students transition from practice and memorization to reasoning?

Rubrics should contain clearly stated descriptions of mastery. Rubrics should also discriminate between each level of performance (Bryant & Driscoll, 1998). The majority of performance tasks address several standards, and within those standards one or more benchmarks apply. The criteria should relate to these benchmarks.

When designing a rubric, teachers should list all criteria that are important to the task and include all concepts and accomplishments crucial to successfully completing the performance. It is imperative to tie the criteria directly to the standards and benchmarks. For example, a geometry standard states that students "specify locations and describe spatial relationships using coordinate geometry and other representational systems," and the benchmark is for students to "make and use coordinate systems to specify locations and to describe paths" (NCTM, 2000, p. 164). The criteria in a rubric should include specifics that provide evidence that students are able to demonstrate understanding of the benchmark. In the case of making a coordinate graph, such a list might include criteria important to the understanding of a graph: a title, labeled and numbered axes, a key (if necessary), and accurately graphed coordinates. Achieving the targeted criteria is the prevailing goal of any task.

The next step is to set the ideal—determine the highest level of quality. Teachers should consider the following questions when determining the ideal performance:

- What does the top level of achievement look like for each criterion?
- How can it be described?

This information should be entered in the greatest numerical level on the rubric and become the expectation for all students.

To complete a rubric, teachers must make decisions regarding the criteria for other levels of performance. Each numerical level should contain a clearly stated description of performance, and each consecutive level should be a step closer to a quality product. In other words, each consecutive level should contain information to bring the product a step closer to the quality desired. Rubrics are tools that guide learners to an exemplary product by defining the levels of expectation with quality descriptors. For a rubric to be an effective tool, it is imperative that the rubric be written in language that students can understand; it should be easy to use and clearly stated, and all levels of performance should build on each other so, when a product is appraised, the evaluator is clear as to where the product fits on the scale.

Before beginning a task, students should be taught how to use the corresponding rubric. They need to clearly understand the expectations. The best way for teachers to do this is to show examples of quality performances while pointing out the corresponding criteria on the rubric. Doing so helps students visualize a top-notch performance. The rubric should be used throughout the task to provide students with clearly articulated performance expectations and to help students maintain focus on the target.

The following Rubric/Mathematics Application targets the standards of numbers and operation, measurement, communication, and problem solving.

RUBRIC/MATHEMATICS APPLICATION

HOW NEGATIVE ARE MY TEMPERATURES?

This application is most appropriate for students who are at an age level where integer operations are taught. Most likely these students will be in Grades 6 through 10. Younger students who need a challenge or who are working at an advanced pace might also find that the application meets their needs. Further suggestions for simplification and extension can be found in the application explanations. An overview of the application is provided in Figure 2.1.

Performance Task Explanation

To complete this application, students should be able to compare integers and add and subtract integers. During the task, students have ample opportunity to practice integer manipulations, demonstrate their own capabilities, and explain the procedures they used when working with integers. This performance task takes about two to three 45-minute class periods.

To begin the performance task, students need to locate and collect the data necessary to complete the task. Because the object of the assignment is to work with integers, students need to search for information about a state that experiences subzero winter temperatures. The data collection process might begin with an Internet search of weather information to locate an appropriate site. This could be done using the keyword *weather*. Students can also e-mail local weather personalities and ask for sites that contain the data required. (If teachers choose to have students do this, they should have students send their e-mail several days before

Figure 2.2

starting the task so that e-mail recipients have time to respond.) Another option is for students to use the Web site listed in the suggested student procedures in the overview. When doing their research, students should search for the daily record high and low temperatures for the month of January. Student findings can be recorded on the organizational chart provided in Figure 2.2, or students may wish to create their own graphic organizer.

After recording data on the chart, students can begin their calculations. The difference between the record high temperature and the record low temperature should be determined for each day of the month. The temperatures should also be compared to find the lowest and highest temperature of the month. Students can show their calculations on a separate piece of paper.

After completing all calculations, students need to explain the procedures used to compare the integers and the methods used to add and subtract integers. Explanations should be written and clear examples should be provided. Students should create their own organizational tool to record this information. Two graphic organizers (Figures 2.3 and 2.4) highlighting the procedures used when adding and subtracting integers are included in this chapter and can be used as teaching tools or examples. These student samples might be best used before beginning the task as a way to help students remember the processes for adding and subtracting integers.

Unit Overview

How Negative Are My Temperatures?

Standards:	Numbers and Operations, Measurement, Communication, Problem Solving
Mathematics concepts:	Compare integers, add and subtract integers
Grade levels:	6 through 10
Related curricular areas:	Technology—Using the Internet; Language Arts—Writing an Explanation
Materials:	Computer with Internet access
Task:	Weather reporters throughout the world are in desperate need of your help. The computer program typically used to determine high and low temperatures and to calculate temperature ranges has been destroyed by a computer virus. Because weather reporters have become so reliant on technology, they no longer remember how to make the calculations necessary to determine the temperatures—especially in cold regions. Their public is waiting; they want information now. The weather reporters need you to research and calculate the temperatures for them. They would also be very grateful if you would explain how you arrived at your answers so they are not helpless should a similar situation happen again in the future.

Suggested Student Procedures

1. Using the Internet, find the record high and low temperatures for January in Wisconsin or another state with extreme winter temperatures. (One possible Web site is www.crh.noaa.gov.)
2. Identify the warmest and the coldest temperature for the month.
3. Find the differences between the record high and record low temperatures for each day of the month.
4. Clearly explain the procedures used for adding and subtracting integers. Give examples. Include an explanation of the method used to compare integers to identify the high and low temperatures for the month.
5. Organize all information on a poster or visual display. You may want to include a calendar, easy-to-understand charts, or graphic organizers (a graphic display of your findings).

Teacher Resources

High and Low Temperature Record Organizer
Adding and Subtracting Integers Student Helpers #1 and #2
Rubric

Checkups 1 and 2 and Answer Keys
Integer Challenge and Key

Internet Resources

Discovery School: Offers homework helpers for students and creative mathematics curriculum resources for teachers. (http://school.discovery.com)

Lycos Zone: Offers an interactive mathematics test students can take online for addition, subtraction, multiplication, or division. (http://bonus.lycos.com/bonus/card/Math_Test_game.html)

Math Goodies: Provides interactive mathematics lessons, homework helpers, puzzles, worksheets and more. (http://www.mathgoodies.com)

Figure 2.1

Figure 2.3   **Figure 2.4**   **Figure 2.5**

Rubric

Students should always be aware of the characteristics of success when beginning an application. To meet and exceed the expectations for the task, students need to be aware of all aspects of the performance, including the grading piece. Each student, or cooperative group of students, needs to have a copy of the rubric before beginning the task. The rubric for this application is based on a 1 to 4 scale (see Figure 2.5). Taking a few minutes of class time to read through the descriptors on the rubric results in higher quality products. Make the 4-point section on the rubric clear to the students so they can confidently aim for the highest level of achievement. Allow students time to ask questions.

When grading the finished products, simply circle or highlight the numerical value that is the most accurate description of the performance. The individual criterion should be added to determine the final score achieved on the rubric.

Expanding the Task

To expand the performance task, ask students to find average temperatures for each week of the month. This requires knowledge of the operations of multiplication and division of decimals. Students should organize and record the information. Students should also be prepared to explain the methods they used to find the average.

Students might also research temperatures in another country and compare them to the temperatures used to complete the original performance task.

Simplifying the Task

To simplify the performance task, have students limit their research and calculations to the first week of the month. Identifying the high temperature and low temperature of 1 week might be a good task for younger students.

Figure 2.6

Shortening the Task

If time is limited, the students can work only on the mathematics aspect of the task. Depending on the age level of the students, completing the research and doing the mathematical calculations can be finished in one or two class

Figure 2.7   **Figure 2.8**   **Figure 2.9**

periods. Students can eliminate the written explanation and the visual display, if necessary. These, however, are important parts of the task and help determine if students fully grasp the concepts involved. The extra time is worth the depth of understanding students gain. Explaining thinking is a metacognitive strategy that helps students clarify their thoughts and solidify their knowledge.

Figure 2.10   **Figure 2.11**

Checkup

The activities in Figures 2.6 and 2.7 can be used as an assignment or an assessment. If used before the performance task, the checkup can determine if the students are ready to complete the task. If used after the task as an assessment, the activity provides another indication of the students' ability to perform computations accurately when asked to add and subtract integers. Keys to these activities are offered in Figures 2.8 to 2.9.

Challenge Activity

The Integer Challenge graphic organizer (see Figure 2.10) can be used as an optional activity for students in need of a bigger challenge. The challenge is in solving equations involving adding and subtracting fraction integers and decimal integers. A key to the challenge is provided in Figure 2.11.

Visual Display

When all parts of the task have been completed, students should organize all task components on a visual display or poster. Comparing the display with the rubric gives students clear expectations for their performance.

IN SUMMARY

Standards provide focus for students' efforts. They provide a clear vision of what it is teachers want students to know and be able to do. Standards offer the target, and it is the teacher's job to point students in the desired direction and create tasks that result in a clear view of the targeted achievement.

How Negative Are My Temperatures?

High and Low Temperature Record Organizer

Write the high and low record temperatures for each day of the month on the line provided. The third line for each day can be used to record the difference between the high and low temperatures.

Month: _____

1 high ____ low ____ ____	**2** high ____ low ____ ____	**3** high ____ low ____ ____	**4** high ____ low ____ ____	**5** high ____ low ____ ____	**6** high ____ low ____ ____	**7** high ____ low ____ ____
8 high ____ low ____ ____	**9** high ____ low ____ ____	**10** high ____ low ____ ____	**11** high ____ low ____ ____	**12** high ____ low ____ ____	**13** high ____ low ____ ____	**14** high ____ low ____ ____
15 high ____ low ____ ____	**16** high ____ low ____ ____	**17** high ____ low ____ ____	**18** high ____ low ____ ____	**19** high ____ low ____ ____	**20** high ____ low ____ ____	**21** high ____ low ____ ____
22 high ____ low ____ ____	**23** high ____ low ____ ____	**24** high ____ low ____ ____	**25** high ____ low ____ ____	**26** high ____ low ____ ____	**27** high ____ low ____ ____	**28** high ____ low ____ ____
29 high ____ low ____ ____	**30** high ____ low ____ ____	**31** high ____ low ____ ____				

Figure 2.2

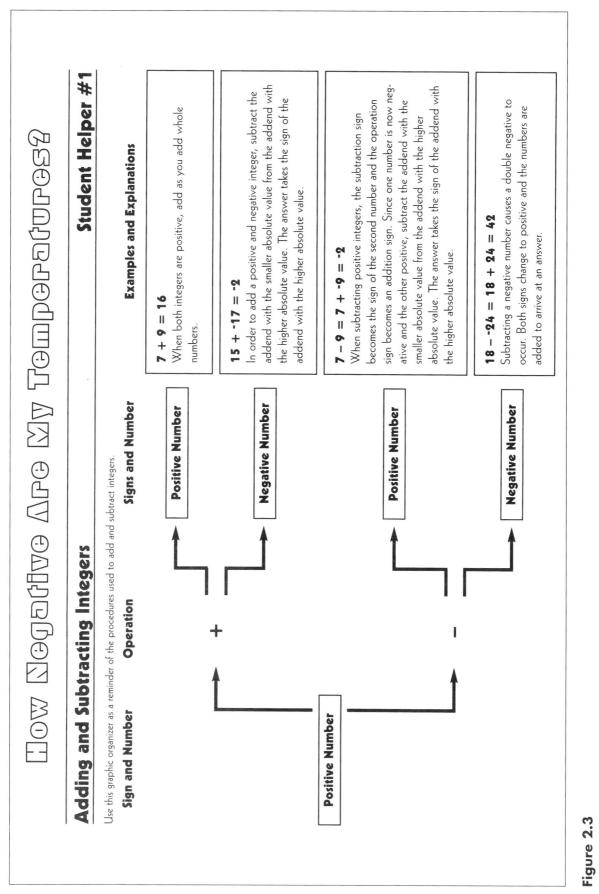

How Negative Are My Temperatures?

Adding and Subtracting Integers

Use this graphic organizer as a reminder of the procedures used to add and subtract integers.

Sign and Number	Operation	Signs and Number	Examples and Explanations

Student Helper #1

Positive Number

Positive Number → + → **Positive Number**

Negative Number

7 + 9 = 16
When both integers are positive, add as you add whole numbers.

15 + -17 = -2
In order to add a positive and negative integer, subtract the addend with the smaller absolute value from the addend with the higher absolute value. The answer takes the sign of the addend with the higher absolute value.

Positive Number

Positive Number → – →

Negative Number

7 – 9 = 7 + -9 = -2
When subtracting positive integers, the subtraction sign becomes the sign of the second number and the operation sign becomes an addition sign. Since one number is now negative and the other positive, subtract the addend with the smaller absolute value from the addend with the higher absolute value. The answer takes the sign of the addend with the higher absolute value.

18 – -24 = 18 + 24 = 42
Subtracting a negative number causes a double negative to occur. Both signs change to positive and the numbers are added to arrive at an answer.

Figure 2.3

How Negative Are My Temperatures?

Adding and Subtracting Integers

Use this graphic organizer as a reminder of the procedures used to add and subtract integers.

Sign and Number   Operation   Signs and Number

Examples and Explanations

-7 + 9 = 2
In order to add a positive and negative integer, subtract the addend with the smaller absolute value from the addend with the higher absolute value. The answer takes the sign of the addend with the higher absolute value.

-15 + -17 = -32
Since both integers are negative, the signs are the same so you add to find the answer. Because both signs are negative, the answer is negative.

-7 – 9 = -7 + -9 = -16
When subtracting a negative integer from a negative integer, the subtraction sign becomes the sign of the second number and the operation sign becomes an addition sign. Since the integers are now the same sign, add to find the answer. The answer will be negative since both addends are negative.

-18 – -24 = -18 + 24 = 6
When subtracting a negative number from a negative number, a double negative occurs in front of the second integer. Those two signs change to positive. The integers' signs are now different. In order to add the positive and negative integers, subtract the addend with the smaller absolute value from the addend with the higher absolute value. The answer takes the sign of the addend with the higher absolute value.

Positive Number

Negative Number

Positive Number

Negative Number

+

−

Negative Number

Figure 2.4

How Negative Are My Temperatures?

Rubric

Instructions: Choose the point value that best describes the performance in each category.

	0 *It's icy!*	**1** *It's very cold!*	**2** *It's getting warmer!*	**3** *Perfect temperature!*	*Points Earned*
Data Organizer Accuracy of Information	Not present or completely inaccurate	Half of the data missing or inaccurate	Data complete, some inaccuracies	Data complete and fully accurate	
Neatness	Sloppy, difficult to read	Can be read with careful concentration	Neat, easy to read	Perfectly formed numbers	
Accuracy of Answers Days 1 to 8	5 to 8 errors in calculations	3 to 4 errors in calculations	1 to 2 errors in calculations	Calculations perfect!	
Days 9 to 16	5 to 8 errors in calculations	3 to 4 errors in calculations	1 to 2 errors in calculations	Calculations perfect!	
Days 17 to 24	5 to 8 errors in calculations	3 to 4 errors in calculations	1 to 2 errors in calculations	Calculations perfect!	
Days 25 to 31	5 to 8 errors in calculations	3 to 4 errors in calculations	1 to 2 errors in calculations	Calculations perfect!	
Explanations Comparing of Integers	Explanation missing	Explanation in need of clarification	Clear, accurate explanation	Clear, accurate explanation, including examples	
Adding Integers	Explanation missing	Explanation in need of clarification	Clear, accurate explanation	Clear, accurate explanation, including examples	
Subtracting Integers	Explanation missing	Explanation in need of clarification	Clear, accurate explanation	Clear, accurate explanation, including examples	
Display	Lacks organization and neatness	Neatly organized, parts missing	Neatly organized, all components present	Neatly organized, attractive display, with all components present	

Points possible = 30   Points earned = _____

Evaluator: _____

Figure 2.5

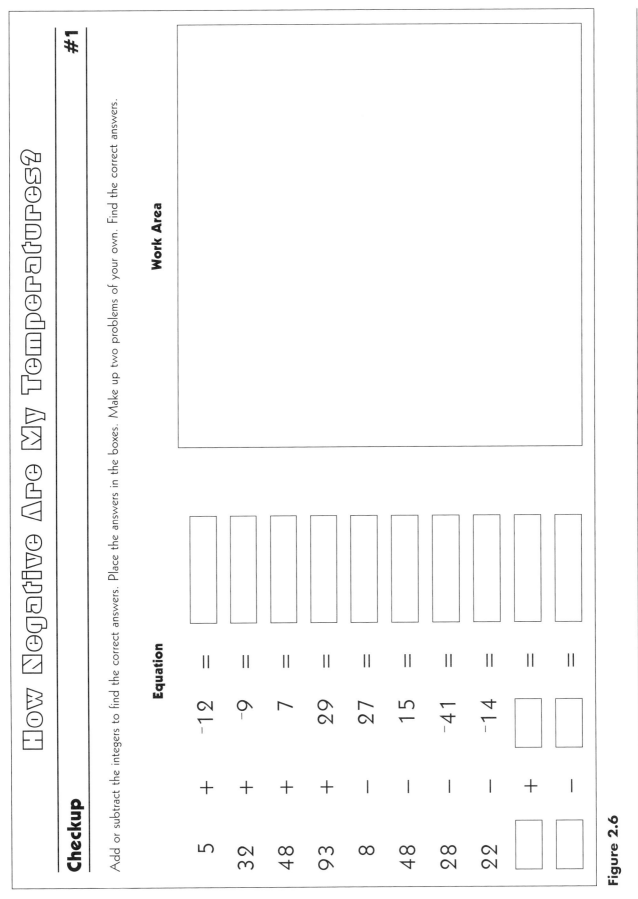

How Negative Are My Temperatures?

Checkup #1

Add or subtract the integers to find the correct answers. Place the answers in the boxes. Make up two problems of your own. Find the correct answers.

Equation

5 + ⁻12 = ☐

32 + ⁻9 = ☐

48 + 7 = ☐

93 + 29 = ☐

8 − 27 = ☐

48 − 15 = ☐

28 − ⁻41 = ☐

22 − ⁻14 = ☐

☐ + ☐ = ☐

☐ − ☐ = ☐

Work Area

Figure 2.6

How Negative Are My Temperatures?

High and Low Temperature Checkup

#2

Add or subtract the integers to find the correct answers. Place the answers in the boxes. Make up two problems of your own. Find the correct answers.

Equation

⁻9 + ⁻62 = ☐

⁻87 + ⁻7 = ☐

⁻48 + 78 = ☐

⁻76 + 79 = ☐

⁻48 − 46 = ☐

⁻39 − 95 = ☐

⁻58 − ⁻45 = ☐

⁻32 − ⁻94 = ☐

☐ + ☐ = ☐

☐ + ☐ = ☐

Work Area

Figure 2.7

How Negative Are My Temperatures?

Checkup – Key

#1

Add or subtract the integers to find the correct answers. Place the answers in the boxes. Make up two problems of your own. Find the correct answers.

Equation

5	+	-12	=	-7
32	+	-9	=	23
48	+	7	=	55
93	+	29	=	122
8	–	27	=	-19
48	–	15	=	33
28	–	-41	=	69
22	–	-14	=	36
	+		=	
	–		=	

Work Area

Figure 2.8

Checkup – Key

Add or subtract the integers to find the correct answers. Place the answers in the boxes. Make up two problems of your own. Find the correct answers.

Equation

-9	+	-62	=	-71
-87	+	-7	=	-94
-48	+	78	=	30
-76	+	79	=	3
-48	–	46	=	-94
-39	–	95	=	-134
-58	–	-45	=	-13
-32	–	-94	=	62
☐	+	☐	=	☐
☐	–	☐	=	☐

Work Area

Figure 2.9

How Negative Are My Temperatures?

Integer Challenge

Solve each equation. Place your answer in the empty box.

Figure 2.10

How Negative re My Temperatures?

Integer Challenge – Key

Solve each equation. Place your answer in the empty box.

⁻7.9	+	**⁻40.4**	=	⁻48.3
⁻10.16	+	3.14	=	⁻7.02
⁻5.61	+	32	=	**26.39**
38	+	⁻5.32	=	**32.68**
⁻0.39	+	**1.39**	=	1

4.3	−	**⁻20.7**	=	25
⁻49.5	−	⁻8.2	=	⁻41.3
5.31	−	7.34	=	⁻2.03
⁻12.96	−	**4.43**	=	⁻17.39
⁻36.36	−	⁻34	=	⁻2.36

$-2\frac{1}{3}$	+	7	=	$\mathbf{4\frac{2}{3}}$
$\frac{-3}{4}$	+	$4\frac{1}{2}$	=	$3\frac{3}{4}$
$\mathbf{-11\frac{3}{10}}$	+	$8\frac{9}{10}$	=	$-2\frac{2}{5}$
$4\frac{2}{7}$	+	$\mathbf{-12\frac{20}{21}}$	=	$-8\frac{2}{3}$
$19\frac{1}{3}$	+	$\mathbf{-46\frac{1}{3}}$	=	⁻27

$4\frac{1}{3}$	−	$\mathbf{-3\frac{1}{2}}$	=	$7\frac{5}{6}$
$-3\frac{1}{2}$	−	$\mathbf{6\frac{1}{4}}$	=	$-9\frac{3}{4}$
$5\frac{4}{5}$	−	$\mathbf{-1\frac{13}{15}}$	=	$7\frac{2}{3}$
$\mathbf{-15\frac{1}{12}}$	−	$-2\frac{3}{4}$	=	$-12\frac{1}{3}$
$\mathbf{26\frac{1}{8}}$	−	$8\frac{7}{8}$	=	$17\frac{1}{4}$

Figure 2.11

3

Performance Tasks and Rubrics

WHY USE PERFORMANCE TASKS?

A performance task is a meaningful measurement of a student's level of understanding of a concept or concepts. Performance tasks relate knowledge to real-world applications. To complete a performance task, students are expected to use their computational skills to reason, communicate, and understand, not to simply reproduce memorized skills and procedures. According to Burke (1999), the key characteristic of performance tasks involves creating real-life applications for real-life problems. With performance tasks, students are asked to apply the skills and concepts they have learned to problem solving, which helps to embed what they have learned. As Burke stated, "By demonstrating what they can do, students have a greater probability of transferring the skills they learned to life rather than merely reproducing knowledge for a test" (p. 79).

Students learn by being actively engaged in the learning process; they learn by doing (Zemelman et al., 1993). In mathematics, this equates to activities such as completing real-world tasks, collecting and analyzing data, and drawing conclusions from discoveries. Giving students the opportunity to perform complex tasks through such real-world applications gives educators new insights into what students are able to do with the skills and knowledge they possess (Caudell, 1996). Performance tasks also help students develop the ability to understand the relationships between concepts and procedures.

Students learn mathematical concepts by working with others to develop solutions to problems and by communicating their ideas and understandings. Such active engagement fosters metacognition and reflection while students are engaged in the task, which helps students better learn the concepts. The more often students engage in a concept, the better they become at that concept and the more likely they are to remember it. This is important because students need to make sense of the concepts to truly understand mathematical procedures. If students simply follow rules and copy formulas established by others, they are not likely to develop the conceptual structure and reasoning skills needed to apply mathematical knowledge to real-world situations (Battista, 1999).

The challenge for teachers is to provide students with opportunities to build mathematical confidence within the classroom so that students discover mathematics and its usefulness. As Crosswaite et al. (1989) stated, mathematics is not a spectator sport; active involvement is the key to understanding.

Black and Wiliam (1998) believe that to support the development of meaningful mathematical tasks, teaching and learning must be interactive and include the following characteristics:

- The development of tasks needs to be clearly tied to the learning aims or standards.
- Students must be provided the opportunity to communicate their evolving understandings during the implementation and developmental stages of a task.
- All students need to have the opportunity to express their ideas, and students need to be encouraged and involved in the thinking process.

CHARACTERISTICS OF PERFORMANCE TASKS

When developing a performance task, the first thing teachers should keep in mind is that it is imperative that any performance task be directly linked to the standards and benchmarks being addressed. The focus of the task should be clear, and expectations should be high. The purpose of the task should be accomplished through its performance.

The next thing teachers should consider is how the task relates to the real world. The task needs to have a real-world connection—it should go beyond isolated calculations and form a bridge between the concepts and their use in everyday life. Problems should be able to be generalized to other situations, and the problem's authenticity should also be apparent. The following questions can help ensure the performance task has a real-world connection:

- Does the task actively engage the learner (i.e., will the learner conduct action research or participate in a hands-on activity to find the solution)?

- Will the task interest the students and does it have connections to their lives?
- Does the task promote higher level thinking (i.e., does it require students to apply knowledge in a creative way)?
- Is there more than one correct answer to the task?

In addition to these characteristics, a real-world performance task should assess higher levels of understanding. The task should provide evidence that students can complete tasks that require complex thinking processes (Schurr, Thomason, & Thomason, 1996).

The scoring system for a performance task is unique and focuses on the task in comparison to the performance. A performance task does not have a single correct answer and cannot be evaluated like a traditional multiple-choice test because it is more complex than a traditional test. With such tasks, students often find multiple ways to demonstrate their understanding and produce the information needed to create a solution. A rubric is the perfect evaluation tool for this type of performance.

It is important to make use of the rubric when evaluating tasks. The rubric provides students with a roadmap to a high-quality performance. Schmoker (2006) indicated that teachers don't use rubrics enough, even when they know their use is effective. Make the commitment to use the rubric for increased success in student demonstration of understanding.

CREATING THE PERFORMANCE TASK

There are several steps teachers can use as guidelines for creating a performance task:

Step 1: Choose the standards, benchmarks, and concepts that the task will measure. Doing this outlines the expected outcomes. When outlining such outcomes, keep the following questions in mind:

- What knowledge should students discover while they are performing the task?
- What skills are necessary to complete the performance?
- What accomplishments are necessary for the task to be considered a success?

Step 2: Develop a situation or real-world connection. Provide a task description in writing when developing the task. Consider the following questions:

- How are the mathematical concepts used in real life?
- What kind of task can extend students' knowledge and encourage mathematical connections to the world outside of the textbook?
- What procedures can actively engage students in a learning experience that puts their skills to use while engaging their brain in extensions of actual mathematical applications?

Step 3: Clearly outline the task by listing suggested procedures for task completion. During this process, keep in mind what students need to do to successfully complete the task.

List the supplies or tools needed for task implementation. It is important to keep costs reasonable; many tasks may not require additional supplies. To make sure all potential supplies are being considered, ask the following questions:

- Are special materials needed that are not typically found in the classroom?
- Who will purchase the items needed?
- Is access to a computer lab essential?

Step 4: Develop a time frame. Some tasks require a class period or two to complete, whereas more extensive tasks can take a few weeks. Make sure that the time commitment is justifiable, considering the concepts being addressed. When developing a time frame, consider the following:

- What is a reasonable length of time for task completion?
- Will the task be completed at school or will the task require time outside of the school day as well?

Step 5: Create a rubric. To create a rubric that fits the task, consider the following questions:

- What criteria are important to the successful completion of the task?
- What does an exemplary level of performance look like?

The Performance Task Planning Guide offered in Figure 3.1 provides an organizer that can be used to determine that all facets are addressed during task development.

Performance Task Planning Guide

STANDARDS AND BENCHMARKS

_____

_____

MATHEMATICS CONCEPTS

_____

_____

TASK DESCRIPTION

_____

_____

_____

_____

SUGGESTED PROCEDURES

_____

_____

_____

_____

_____

_____

_____

SUPPLIES AND SPECIAL NEEDS

_____

_____

TIME FRAME

_____

_____

ASSESSMENT TOOL

_____

_____

Figure 3.1

RUBRIC/MATHEMATICS APPLICATION

LET'S GO SHOPPING!

This application in this chapter centers on whole number and decimal operations. The real-world application, in this case, is shopping. From the time children are quite young, they realize that money is a necessary commodity if they want to obtain something. In school, they learn to add, subtract, multiply, and divide. This task turns students into consumers. They are given a budget and a purpose. It is their job to spend money responsibly, account for what they spend, and buy with a purpose. Students enjoy this task because they can shop and "spend money" at no cost.

An overview of the application is provided in Figure 3.2.

Figure 3.3

Performance Task Explanation

Students are "given" $42 to spend on each family member for an upcoming event or holiday. Students who have small families might want to include extended family members. Students with large families may want to make purchases for a limited number of people. Groups of three to eight members work well depending on the age level of the students completing the task. This task takes about two to three 45-minute class periods to complete. A task explanation that can be given to students is provided in Figure 3.3.

Using a variety of catalogs and newspaper ads, students should find gifts for each family member. Pictures of each gift should be neatly cut out and glued onto a gift display page. Each gift should be labeled with the price and the name of the family member to whom it will belong. A sample of the gift display page is shown in Figure 3.4.

Figure 3.4

Time limits will probably be needed for this part of the activity. Students will find they like to shop, and without some time structure this part of the performance task could go on for a long time. Giving students one class period to shop is a good option. Encourage discussion during the gift selection process. Ask students to share their shopping strategies, discuss how they intend to spend their money, and compare prices with others in the class. All of these discussions are learning experiences for the students.

Upon completion of the gift display page, students should determine the total amount spent for each family member by filling out the Level 1 Receipt and Calculations page (see Figure 3.5). To make the task more difficult, teachers can use the Level 2 Receipt and Calculations form (see Figure 3.6), which asks students to calculate the tax for each individual item purchased.

All computations should be written on the form. Because one purpose of this activity is to increase computational skills,

Figure 3.5

Unit Overview

Let's Go Shopping!

Standards:	Numbers and Operations, Problem Solving, Communication, Connections
Mathematics concepts:	Whole number and decimal operations
Grade levels:	3 to 9
Related curricular areas:	Art—creating a display page; language arts—writing an explanation
Materials needed:	Catalogs and newspaper ads
Task:	Your family has a large celebration coming up and you need to buy gifts for everyone. You have been given a total of $42 per person to spend. You want to make sure that everyone gets at least two items.

Suggested Student Procedures

1. Using catalogs and ads, find gifts for your family members (including yourself). Buy at least two gifts per person, spending as close to $42 for each person as possible.

2. Cut out pictures of each item you want to purchase. Create a display of each item and its price. Indicate which family member the gift is for.

3. For each family member, create a receipt, including an item description and price, as well as the total spent for that person.

4. Determine the total amount spent on gifts.

5. Complete the reflections page.

6. Make a folder or cover to hold your project. Include the gift display page, the receipts and calculations page, the reflections page, the rubric, and your checklist.

Teacher Resources

Task Explanation and Suggested Procedures page

Sample Gift Display

Receipt and Calculations page, Levels 1 and 2

Reflections Page and Sample Key

Rubric

Checklist

Internet Resources

FunBrain: Students can take part in an interactive Math Baseball game involving addition, subtraction, multiplication, and division, or all of these. (www.funbrain.com/math/)

A+ Math: This site helps students improve their mathematics skills interactively by offering flash cards, games, homework helpers, and worksheets. (http://www.aplusmath.com)

Do Math . . . and you can do anything: This site contains activities involving real-life mathematics challenges for students and families. (http://www.domath.org)

Figure 3.2

Figure 3.6

calculators should not be used. Partner checking is an option to increase computational accuracy. To calculate the total amount spent, students can add the money spent on each individual member. More than one copy of the Receipts and Calculations sheet will be needed for each student so students can include the information for all of their family members. To calculate the total budget, students can multiply the number of family members by $42. By subtracting the total spent from the total budget, students determine the amount of money remaining.

The Reflections page (see Figure 3.7) can be completed as students finish other portions of the task. The Reflections page helps students to embed their learning by asking them to reflect on and consider the choices they made. An example of a student response to this Reflection page is provided in Figure 3.8. After completing the Reflection, students can create a cover for their work using a folder to organize and house the completed items.

Figure 3.7   **Figure 3.8**   **Figure 3.9**   **Figure 3.10**

Rubric

Distribute the rubric (see Figure 3.9) with the task explanation and suggested procedures. The performance task needs to be clearly explained, and the rubric will aid understanding of the task. Direct students to look at the criteria in the left column of the rubric. Read the descriptors for the 3-point column to make students aware of the level of expected quality. Students can refer to the rubric throughout the process for a reminder of the level of quality they should be working toward.

Checklist

Students can use the checklist in Figure 3.10 to determine if they have finished all of the necessary steps for successful task completion before turning in their projects. This checklist contains many of the same criteria found in the rubric.

IN SUMMARY

Performance tasks can be a catalyst for understanding. Skill repetition results in memorization, whereas performance tasks inspire thinking. Relating mathematics to real-world applications is a constructive way to bring purpose to the mathematics classroom and to help students apply their mathematics skills to solve real problems. Actively engaging students in learning helps them form connections and transfer their skills to new situations, which results in the meaningful use of skills and the extension of in-depth knowledge.

Let's Go Shopping!

Task Explanation and Suggested Procedures

Task:

Your family has a large celebration coming up, and you need to buy gifts for everyone. You have been given $42 per person to spend. You want to make sure that everyone gets at least two items.

Suggested Procedures:

1. Using catalogs and ads, find gifts for your family members (including yourself). Buy at least two gifts per person, spending as close to $42 for each person as possible.

2. Cut out pictures of each item you want to purchase. Create a display including each item and its price. Indicate which family member the gift is for.

3. For each family member, create a receipt, including an item description and price, as well as the total spent for that person.

4. Determine the total amount spent on gifts.

5. Complete the reflections page.

6. Make a folder or cover to hold your project. Include the gift display page, the receipts and calculations page, the reflections page, the rubric, and your checklist.

Figure 3.3

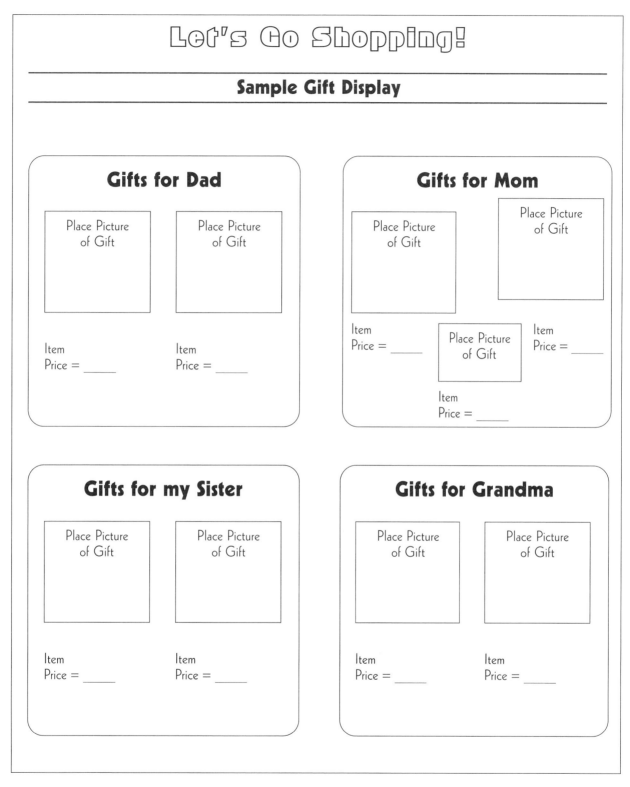

Figure 3.4

Let's Go Shopping!

Receipts and Calculations   **Level 1**

Total Budget = _____

Family Member:	
Item	**Cost**
Total	

Family Member:	
Item	**Cost**
Total	

Family Member:	
Item	**Cost**
Total	

Family Member:	
Item	**Cost**
Total	

Family Member:	
Item	**Cost**
Total	

Family Member	**Amount Spent**
Grand Total	

Figure 3.5

Let's Go Shopping!

Receipts and Calculations

Level 2

Total Budget = _____

Family Member:

Item	Cost	Tax	Total

Total

Family Member:

Item	Cost	Tax	Total

Total

Family Member	Amount Spent

Grand Total

Figure 3.6

Let's Go Shopping!

Reflections

Choose one of the gifts you selected. Why did you decide to buy it?

_____

_____

_____

_____

What mathematical skills did you use to complete this project?

_____

_____

_____

_____

Did you compare prices from different catalogs or ads? What would be the benefit of making price comparisons?

_____

_____

_____

_____

What did you learn while completing this task?

_____

_____

_____

_____

Figure 3.7

Let's Go Shopping!

Reflections – Sample Key

Choose one of the gifts you selected. Why did you decide to buy it?

I thought my mom would like a wallet and it was on sale.

What mathematical skills did you use to complete this project?

I added and subtracted to find out how much I spent and the money I could still spend.

Did you compare prices from different catalogs or ads? What would be the benefit of making price comparisons?

Some things I couldn't compare because it was only in one ad. I did compare the toys because they were in two ads, and I could save money by taking the cheaper price.

What did you learn while completing this task?

It's not easy to shop for everyone when you have a budget. You really need to watch what you spend your money on.

Figure 3.8

Let's Go Shopping!

Rubric

Instructions: Highlight the box for each category that best describes the performance. Add points together to determine the rubric score.

	0	1	2	3
Cover	Not present or incomplete	Complete	Complete, neat	Complete, neat, includes project task explanations
Items Display page Pictures	Not present or incomplete	Complete	Complete, labeled with family's names	Complete, labeled with family's names, neat
Prices	Not present or incomplete	Complete	Complete, includes decimal point and $	Complete, includes decimal point and $, neatly written
Appearance	Sloppy	Lacks organization	Organized	Organized and attractive
Receipts and Calculations page Names and Numbers	Not present	Incomplete	Complete	Complete and neatly written
Calculations	Not present or 3 or more incorrect	2 incorrect	1 incorrect	All correct
Budget	Not present	Inaccurate	Accurate	Accurate and clearly labeled
Reflections	Not present	Present	Present, well thought out answers	Present, well thought out answers, complete sentences, accurate spelling

Evaluator: _____   Points possible = 24   Points earned = _____

Figure 3.9

Let's Go Shopping!

Checklist

Directions: Compare your project to the checklist. Put an *X* in the columns that show what you have completed.

	YES!	Not there yet.
Project Packaging		
Booklet cover or folder		
Items Display page		
Pictures displayed		
Prices listed		
Decimals accurately placed		
Orderly appearance		
Organized		
Receipts and Calculations		
Names and numbers neatly written		
Calculations accurate		
Total budget listed		
Reflections		
Complete sentences		
Accurate spelling		
Well-thought-out answers		

Figure 3.10

4

Developing the Rubric From a Checklist

THE CHECKLIST

In the world of education, a checklist is an educational shopping list that indicates the criteria teachers are looking (or shopping) for in a student product or performance, the goal of the task presented to students, and the requirements and expectations of the task. Checklists are the first step in developing a rubric. The checklist is also a tool to be used by students after finishing a project to determine whether or not they have completed all portions of the task. Although checklists do not necessarily speak to quality, they do give students a clear picture of what still needs to be completed before they give their project to the teacher. Although checklists can be used for grading, they do not have the same impact as rubrics because checklists do not measure the quality of the work as rubrics do.

Teachers can use benchmarks to discern which parts of the task are most important, and teachers can highlight these tasks in the checklist. Benchmarks provide such guidance because they outline the criteria the district deems important and necessary for various subject areas. To create an appropriate checklist, teachers should first list the task criteria, making sure to include everything important to a successful task outcome. The checklist should create a visual reminder of all that is crucial in the final product and should be based on observable criteria. A checklist must include the following components:

- a list of criteria or components that need to be included in a finished product,
- a column indicating completion of the components, and
- a column indicating the student has yet to complete the components.

Although a checklist can be a valuable tool, it has limitations. The checklist indicates whether a benchmark has been addressed, but the checklist does not speak to quality, and quality is the ultimate goal. The main difference between a checklist and a rubric is that a rubric describes quality, whereas a checklist simply indicates whether a component has been included. A checklist reminds students what they are expected to include in a completed piece of work; a rubric gives students a clear picture of the expectations of an exemplary performance. For a simple checklist to evolve into a rubric, a transition must take place.

THE TRANSITION FROM CHECKLIST TO RUBRIC

A checklist provides clear criteria that are important to the completion of a task or performance. Using those criteria, the teacher can develop a rubric to evaluate quality and understanding. The criteria outlined in the checklist are expanded in the rubric to include various levels of performance. The rubric should include precise performance expectations and provide students with a description of what the performance looks like. Rubrics also should clearly indicate expectations, state targets, and describe evaluation criteria.

The rubrics used in each Rubric/Mathematics Application in this book are analytic rubrics. These rubrics were designed to evaluate a product as part of the formative process. Holistic rubrics are more summative, are not easily used as part of the growth process, and are typically used as a final evaluation of a product or performance. As discussed in Chapter 1, analytic rubrics tend to give students feedback that is specific to their tasks and can be incorporated into the development process as both learning and evaluation tools. Danielson (1997) recommends analytic rubrics for classroom use, instead of holistic rubrics, because of the feedback analytic rubrics provide. This feedback helps students improve their performance because it provides information regarding specific expectations and gives descriptors that clearly outline what is needed for a higher level of performance.

Three basic steps are necessary to create a rubric. Step 1 is developing the checklist. The checklist becomes the criteria used for the rubric. Figure 4.1 shows a commonly used format for a rubric.

After listing the criteria, teachers need to make decisions regarding point value. Although the rubrics found in the Rubric/Mathematics Applications in this book are 4-point rubrics, there is room for flexibility when creating point systems. However, there are some guidelines that

Criteria	Point Values	Descriptions of Quality			

Figure 4.1

teachers should consider during rubric development. If there are too many levels to a rubric, it becomes difficult to distinguish the difference between levels, and the rubric also becomes increasingly complicated for students to use. If there are too few levels, room for growth or expansion within the levels may not be well represented.

Step 2 in creating a rubric is to develop the point scale for the rubric. An even number of points works well because there is no rubric middle, or center point. (With an odd number of points there is always a middle; e.g., with 5 points, 3 is the middle point.) In rubric grading, teachers sometimes have a tendency to choose the center point value. If there is no center, teachers use the descriptors more effectively and rely on the information stated for each level of the criteria.

After the point scale is chosen, teachers need to decide if a 0 or a 1 should be used as the lowest level of the rubric. In some cases, the lowest level of the rubric indicates little to no evidence of the expected criteria. In this case, a 0 may be more appropriate than a 1. (If the student showed little or no evidence of the expected criteria but received a 1 for these areas, the point total may not indicate that no evidence of the criteria was shown.) A 1 is typically used as the lowest level of the rubric when minimal evidence is shown that a student understands a concept or application component. If 1 is the lowest point value used for the rubric, 0 can be absent yet be an understood possibility for no evidence of a performance. When the lowest level of the rubric is 1, students can also be told that their performance is not complete until they have shown evidence they have met rubric criteria at all categories.

Teachers also need to decide if the point value should be listed from lowest to highest or highest to lowest. The rubrics in this book list the point value from lowest to highest because this allows students to see the point values as a step-by-step process leading up to the ultimate performance.

When rubrics are organized this way, the point values are written like building blocks, with each one building on the one before.

After point scale preferences are chosen, teachers complete Step 3—writing descriptors for each level. It is imperative that descriptors be clear and precise and that the vocabulary used be appropriate to the age level of students who will be using, or who will be evaluated by, the rubric. Starting at the highest level of quality, expectations for each of the criterion should be described. Some questions teachers can consider when developing expectations include

- How is an exemplary product or performance best described?
- What is the evidence of quality? (Be as specific as possible.)

Using previously completed student tasks can be helpful when determining levels of quality. Completed tasks can be used as guides to or reminders of which factors make up an exemplary performance and which factors constitute a lower score. Descriptors should not overlap levels but rather should act as a subsequent step for each level. Descriptors often build on the previous level of performance, and this helps students and evaluators easily determine which level is an appropriate reflection of products or performances.

Although a rubric is a valuable tool that students can use as a guide to a higher level of quality, it is also a piece of work that is under construction. As the rubric is used, it will become apparent if editing is necessary, and adjustments can be made as necessary.

SUMMARY OF STEPS FOR DEVELOPING A RUBRIC

The three basic steps for developing a rubric were outlined in the previous paragraphs. The following figures provide a closer look at rubric development through each step in the process.

Step 1: Develop a Checklist and Rubric Criteria From the Checklist

The checklist in Figure 4.2 was developed for a graphing project from district benchmarks based on the National Council of Teachers of Mathematics (NCTM) standard, "All students should select, create, and use appropriate graphical representations of data" (NCTM, 2000, p. 248).

The rubric in Figure 4.3 is based on the geometry standard, and the benchmark deals with students' ability to design a graph. When developing the list of criteria or components, the teacher should keep in mind the components that need to be included for successful completion of the product. The criterion listed in this rubric corresponds to the benchmarks listed in the checklist in Figure 4.2.

Checklist for a Rubric	YES!	Not yet.
Does the graph have a title?		
Does each axis have a label or title?		
Is the x-axis numbered accurately or is the proper information supplied?		
Is the y-axis numbered accurately?		
Is there a key present?		
Is the information graphed according to the key?		
Is the information graphed accurately?		

Figure 4.2

Developing Rubric Criteria				
Does the graph have a title?				
Does each axis have a label or title?				
Is the x-axis numbered accurately or is the proper information supplied?				
Is the y-axis numbered accurately?				
Is there a key present?				
Is the information graphed according to the key?				
Is the information graphed accurately?				

Figure 4.3

Step 2: Develop the Point System for Each Criterion

The next step in the process is to develop a point system for the rubric. It is important to use a point system that has enough descriptors to properly evaluate the product and few enough so that it is easy for students to use and understand (see Figure 4.4).

Developing a Point System				
	0	**1**	**2**	**3**
Does the graph have a title?				
Does each axis have a label or title?				
Is the x-axis numbered accurately or is the proper information supplied?				
Is the y-axis numbered accurately?				
Is there a key present?				
Is the information graphed according to the key?				
Is the information graphed accurately?				

Figure 4.4

Step 3: Develop the Descriptors for Each Level of Quality

Once a point system is in place, a descriptor for each level of quality should be developed. Descriptors should be written using words that students are familiar with. For the rubric to affect student performance, students must be able to understand it. Descriptors for the highest level of quality should be developed first. This level indicates a top-notch performance and is the highest level of quality. The developer can then work backward from that point, deciding which criteria make up the descending point values. Once all descriptors have been filled in, the rubric is complete and ready to use (see Figure 4.5).

	0	1	2	3
Does the graph have a title?	Not titled	Partially or inaccurately titled	Title present but with errors	Titled accurately
Does each axis have a label or title?	Not titled	Titles present but inappropriate	Titles present but with errors	Titled accurately
Is the x-axis numbered accurately or is the proper information supplied?	Not labeled or numbered	Label or numbers present but inappropriate	Label or numbers present but with errors	Labeled or numbered accurately
Is the y-axis numbered accurately?	Not labeled or numbered	Label or numbers present but inappropriate	Label or numbers present but with errors	Labeled or numbered accurately
Is there a key present?	Not present	Present but incomplete	Present with inaccuracies	Present and accurate
Is the information graphed according to the key?	No correspondence	Much graphed inaccurately	Graphed with minor error	Graphed according to the key
Is the information graphed accurately?	Graph incomplete	Graph complete with several errors	Graph complete with 1 or 2 errors	Graph complete and accurate

Figure 4.5

RUBRIC/MATHEMATICS APPLICATION

WHAT'S MY AREA?

The following application allows students to extend their geometric knowledge by finding the area of an unusual shape. This application contains a checklist and a rubric. A comparison of the two demonstrates how a checklist can be used as a foundational piece for a rubric. An overview of the application is offered in Figure 4.6.

Performance Task Explanation

Students create an unusual shape and find its area. During this process it will become obvious to students that by dividing an unusual shape into smaller geometric shapes the area can be computed with relative ease. This task helps students extend their knowledge of the use of formulas in finding area to a higher level of performance. This task can typically be completed in four 45-minute periods for a fifth- or sixth-grade class—less time is needed for older students and more time for younger students.

Students draw and cut out a combination of eight rectangles, triangles, parallelograms, and trapezoids from various colors of construction paper or other brightly colored paper. Then students glue the shapes onto a large piece of poster paper. Sides of the shapes should be aligned but not overlapping (see Figure 4.7). Students measure and number each shape for identification purposes. They need to determine the location of the base and height of each shape and measure each to the nearest centimeter. Measurements should be accurately recorded on each shape. For organizational purposes, students should record all necessary information on the chart provided in Figure 4.8.

Figure 4.7   **Figure 4.8**

The area of each individual shape should be calculated. After finding the areas of each shape, students add the areas together to discover the area of their creations. To provide evidence of understanding, students should write an explanation of the process they used to find the entire area. That process should be related to the original problem of finding the area of an unusual shape.

 Figure 4.9   **Figure 4.10**   **Figure 4.11**

To make the task cohesive and organized, all information should be neatly placed on a poster board or piece of construction paper. Information should be sensibly organized in a logical fashion so that anyone looking at the poster can determine the information and procedures used to find the area of the irregular shape created by the student (see Figure 4.9 for an example).

Rubric

The rubric (Figure 4.10) should be distributed to students before the task begins. This makes students aware of the task expectations before beginning the performance task. The Task Explanation and Suggested Procedures page (see Figure 4.11) can also be distributed at this time. This page provides students with a copy of the problem as

Unit Overview

What's My Area?

Standards: Measurement, Problem Solving, Communication, Connections

Mathematics concepts: Area of rectangles, triangles, parallelograms, and trapezoids

Grade levels: 2 through 10

Related curricular areas: Language arts—writing explanations; art—creating a poster

Materials: Assorted colors of construction paper, scissors, glue, poster board or large construction paper, rulers

Task: Andre Pentagon, a popular architect, creates houses with unusual shapes. He combines various geometric shapes to create unique rooms. This is a problem for the carpet layers who are working on his current house. They do not know how to calculate the area of the house and cannot determine the amount of carpeting needed. You need to teach the carpet layers how to determine the area of these unusual houses.

Suggested Student Procedures

Create an unusual shape consisting of a variety of geometric shapes. Combine rectangles, triangles, parallelograms, and trapezoids. Follow the following procedures:

1. Choose eight or more pieces of construction paper no smaller than 12 cm by 12 cm each.

2. Using scissors and a ruler, draw and cut two rectangles, two triangles, two parallelograms, and two trapezoids. Each shape should have different dimensions.

3. Number each shape. Measure the base and height of each shape to the nearest centimeter. Write the measurement in the appropriate location on each shape.

4. Align the sides of the shapes in any layout desired. Do not overlap shapes. Glue the pieces onto construction paper to create one large shape out of the smaller pieces.

5. Find the area of each individual shape using the measurements and the proper formulas. Find the area of the larger shape. Use the chart provided to record all information.

6. Write an explanation of the process used to find the area of the irregular shape created. Include an explanation regarding how this applies to the work of the carpet layers.

7. Organize your work on a poster. Include the shape created, the chart, and an explanation of the procedures used.

Teacher Resources

Example Shape page
Organizational Chart
Project Layout Example page
Task Explanation and
    Suggested Procedures page
Rubric
Student Helper page
Checkup and Key

Internet Resources

Interactive Mathematics Miscellany and Puzzles: Features information on mathematics including logic games and puzzles, proofs, web polls, and links to other mathematics sites. (http://www.cut-the-knot.com/content.html)

Math Pop Quiz: Cool quiz network site that includes quizzes on complementary, supplementary, corresponding, and exterior angles. (http://www.mathpopquiz.com)

Professor Freedman's Math Tips: Mathematics strategies for teacher and students including ways to help students deal with mathematics anxiety, study skills and fun resources. (http://www.mathpower.com)

Figure 4.6

well as suggested procedures for accomplishing the task. The problem and procedures should be discussed and questions answered. Flexibility is important; if necessary, procedures should be adjusted to meet the needs of students.

The rubric used for this task is based on a 4-point scale and is a weighted rubric, which means that concepts or performances viewed as more crucial to the understanding of the task are given additional value or weight. (For more information on weighted rubrics, see Chapter 5.) For an example of how to determine scores on a weighted rubric, look at the calculations category on the rubric in Figure 4.11. It has a weight of $\times$ 3. If a student earns 2 points in this category, the points are multiplied by the value of 3. Therefore, the student earns 6 points in this category.

Taking a few minutes of class time to highlight the highest expectations results in products of elevated quality. The 4-point section on the rubric should be clear to the students so they can aim for the top level of achievement. In the case of a weighted rubric, students should also be aware of the weight that corresponds to each criterion.

When tasks are finished and the individual scores for each rubric criterion have been determined, simply add all of the individual scores together. If it is necessary to turn the rubric score into a percent, divide the points earned by the total points possible. The grading scale will vary depending on class procedures. Students should be encouraged to self- and peer-assess before turning in their projects to the teacher. It is beneficial to give students the opportunity to improve scores after the rubric has been completed. This practice heightens student performance and level of achievement.

Figure 4.12

Student Helper

Students may be given a copy of the Student Helper tool (see Figure 4.12). This worksheet helps students identify the proper formula when finding the individual areas.

Figure 4.13

Expanding the Task

Expanding the performance task can be accomplished in any way that fits the mathematics curriculum being taught. For example, students can find the area of circles; squares; obtuse, acute, scalene, and isosceles triangles; and so forth. The number of shapes used can be increased to add to the level of difficulty. Students can also brainstorm their own procedures and create their own organizational tools to complete the task.

Figure 4.14

Simplifying the Task

The performance task can be simplified for younger students by limiting the types of geometric shapes used to one or two. Students might use only rectangles, for example. In this case, each rectangle should be of different dimensions.

Checkup

This optional activity is designed to be used as an assessment. This activity is modeled after the original task but has an increased level of difficulty. In the assessment provided in Figure 4.13, students are asked to find the area of an unusual shape, which is comprised of a combination of trapezoids, rectangles, parallelograms, and triangles. Students are only able to see the outline of the unusual shape and must divide it into geometric shapes, make the appropriate measurements, and create an organizational tool to record the information needed to complete the task. This chart can be similar to the one used in the students' original task and should include formulas, measurements, calculations, and total area.

For some students, this task may be quite difficult. If simplification is required, assist students when they divide the unusual shape or create the divisions before duplicating the assessment for students. The divisions can be drawn on the master copy.

An answer key is located on Figure 4.14. Students may find other ways to divide the shape, but the total area should be within a few centimeters of the area provided on the answer key.

IN SUMMARY

The first step in creating a rubric is to create a checklist. The checklist should clearly state the criteria crucial to the task. After determining the point values, descriptors should be created that illustrate each level of performance. Finally, the rubric is put to the test by trying it with students. Rubrics can always be considered "under construction"—teachers should adjust them as necessary to meet their needs and the needs of their students.

What's My Area?

Example Shape

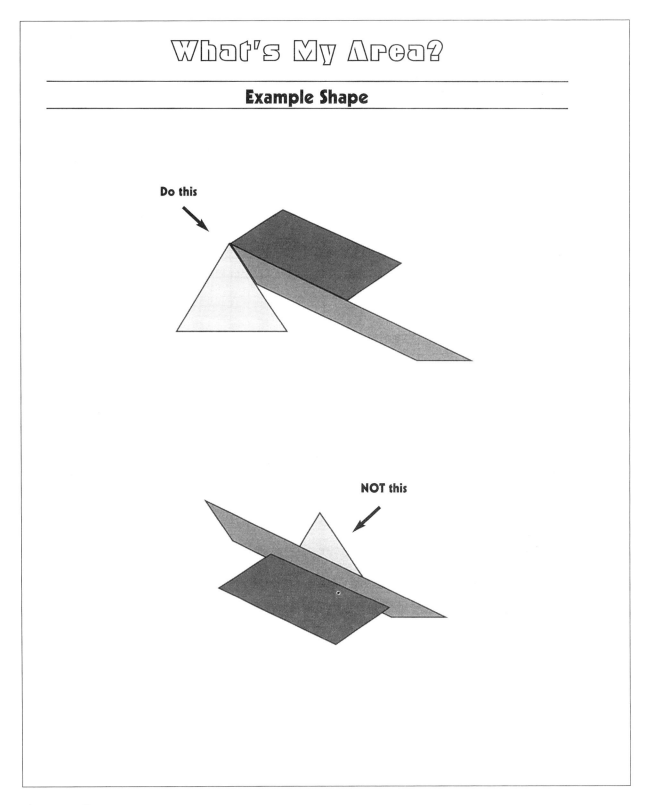

Figure 4.7

What's My Area?

Organizational Chart

Instructions: Complete the chart using the shapes and measurements from the unusual shape you created.

Number and Shape	Formula	Measurements in Formula	Calculations	Area

Total Area = _____

Figure 4.8

What's My Area?

Project Layout Example

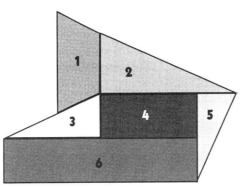

Number and Shape	Formula	Measurements in Formula	Calculations	Area
1. trapezoid	$\left(\dfrac{b_1+b_2}{2}\right)h = A$			
2. triangle	$\dfrac{b \times h}{2} = A$			
3. triangle	$\dfrac{b \times h}{2} = A$			
4. rectangle	$b \times h = A$			
5. triangle	$\dfrac{b \times h}{2} = A$			
6. rectangle	$b \times h = A$			

Total Area = _____

Explanation: In order to find the area of the total shape, it was necessary to find the area of each individual shape using the proper formulas and measurements. After finding the area of each shape, I added the six areas together to arrive at the area of the unusual shape.

If the carpet layers need to find the area of an unusually shaped house, they should first divide the house into shapes they are able to find the area of. Using the proper formulas they can find the areas of the individual units then add them together to find the area of the house.

Figure 4.9

What's My Area?

Rubric

Instructions: Determine which description best fits the completed task for every category on the rubric. Place the earned point value on the line in the last column and multiply by the weight to compute each score. Add scores together to calculate the final score.

	1	2	3	4	
Geometric shapes Shapes	A combination of 1–3 rectangles, triangles, trapezoids, and parallelograms are present and neatly numbered.	A combination of 4–5 rectangles, triangles, trapezoids, and parallelograms are present and neatly numbered.	A combination of 6–7 rectangles, triangles, trapezoids, and parallelograms are present and neatly numbered.	A combination of 8 or more rectangles, triangles, trapezoids, and parallelograms are present and neatly numbered.	___ × 2 = ___
Base and height	1–3 shapes have the base and height accurately and neatly labeled.	4–5 shapes have the base and height accurately and neatly labeled.	6–7 shapes have the base and height accurately and neatly labeled.	8 or more shapes have the base and height accurately and neatly labeled.	___ × 2 = ___
Organizational chart Shapes named and numbered	1–3 shapes are accurately numbered and identified by name on the chart.	4–5 shapes are accurately numbered and identified by name on the chart.	6–7 shapes are accurately numbered and identified by name on the chart.	8 or more shapes are accurately numbered and identified by name on the chart.	___ × 1 = ___
Formulas	1–3 formulas are present and accurate for the corresponding shape.	4–5 formulas are present and accurate for the corresponding shape.	6–7 formulas are present and accurate for the corresponding shape.	8 or more formulas are present and accurate for the corresponding shape.	___ × 2 = ___
Calculations	1–3 calculations are present and accurate for the corresponding shape.	4–5 calculations are present and accurate for the corresponding shape.	6–7 calculations are present and accurate for the corresponding shape.	8 or more calculations are present and accurate for the corresponding shape.	___ × 3 = ___
Area	1–3 areas are correctly computed and labeled with the square unit.	4–5 areas are correctly computed and labeled with the square unit.	6–7 areas are correctly computed and labeled with the square unit.	8 or more areas are correctly computed and labeled with the square unit.	___ × 1 = ___
Written explanation	Difficult to understand.	Clearly written, contains 3 or more spelling or grammatical errors.	Clearly written, contains 1–2 spelling or grammatical errors.	Clearly written, with perfect spelling and punctuation.	___ × 2 = ___
Poster or display	Incomplete or lacks neatness.	Complete, neat.	Complete, neat, and organized.	Complete, well organized, and attractive.	___ × 1 = ___

Evaluator: _____   Points possible = 56   Points earned = _____

Figure 4.10

What's My Area?

Task Explanation and Suggested Procedures

Task:

Andre Pentagon, a popular architect, creates houses with unusual shapes. He combines various geometric shapes to create rooms unlike any others. This has created a problem for the carpet layers who are working on his current house. They do not know how to calculate the area of the house and are unable to determine the amount of carpeting needed. Your help is needed. You need to teach the carpet layers how to determine the area of these unusual houses.

Suggested Procedures:

Create an unusual shape consisting of a variety of geometric shapes. Use a combination of rectangles, triangles, parallelograms, and trapezoids. Follow these procedures:

1. Choose eight or more pieces of construction paper no smaller than 12 cm by 12 cm each.

2. Using scissors and a ruler, draw and cut two rectangles, two triangles, two parallelograms, and two trapezoids. Each shape should have different dimensions.

3. Number each shape. Measure the base and height of each shape to the nearest centimeter. Write the measurement in the appropriate location on each shape.

4. Align the sides of the shapes in any layout desired. Do not overlap shapes. Glue the pieces onto construction paper to create one large shape out of the smaller pieces.

5. Find the area of each individual shape using the measurements and the proper formulas. Find the area of the larger shape. Use the chart provided to record all information.

6. Write an explanation of the process used to find the area of the irregular shape created. Include an explanation of how this applies to the work of the carpet layers.

7. Organize your work on a poster. Include the shape created, the chart, and an explanation of the procedures used.

Figure 4.11

What's My Area?

Student Helper **How Do I Find the Area?**

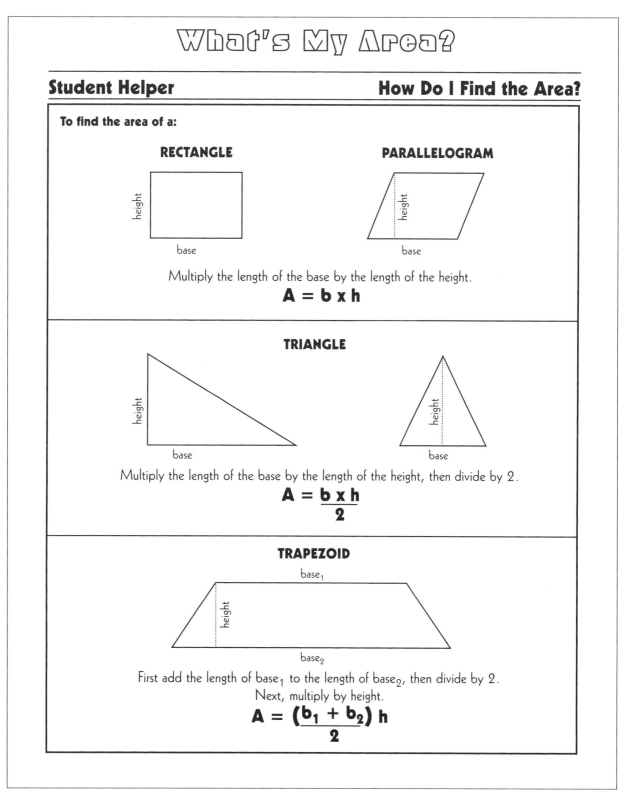

To find the area of a:

RECTANGLE **PARALLELOGRAM**

Multiply the length of the base by the length of the height.

$$A = b \times h$$

TRIANGLE

Multiply the length of the base by the length of the height, then divide by 2.

$$A = \frac{b \times h}{2}$$

TRAPEZOID

First add the length of base$_1$ to the length of base$_2$, then divide by 2.
Next, multiply by height.

$$A = \frac{(b_1 + b_2)\, h}{2}$$

Figure 4.12

What's My Area?

Checkup

Find the area of the shape below. Place any necessary measurements directly on the shape. Measurements should be made to the nearest half of a centimeter (.5 cm). Create a chart to organize all information needed to find the area. Include all formulas, calculations, and areas used to determine the area of the unusual shape.

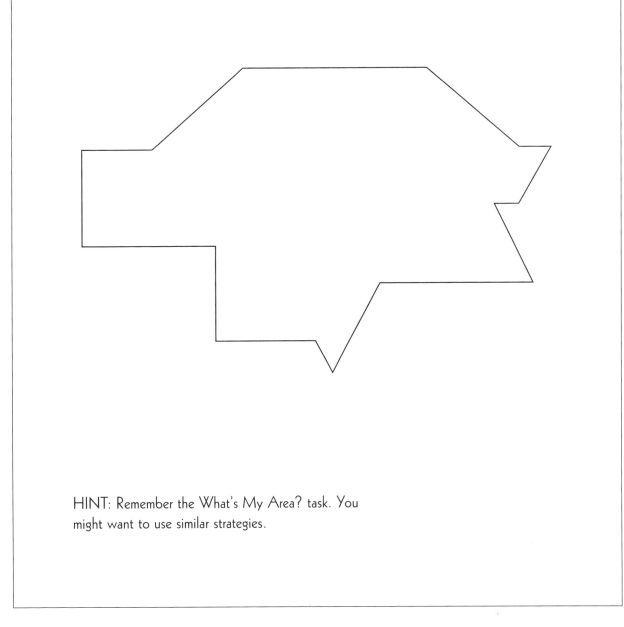

HINT: Remember the What's My Area? task. You might want to use similar strategies.

Figure 4.13

What's My Area?

Checkup – Key

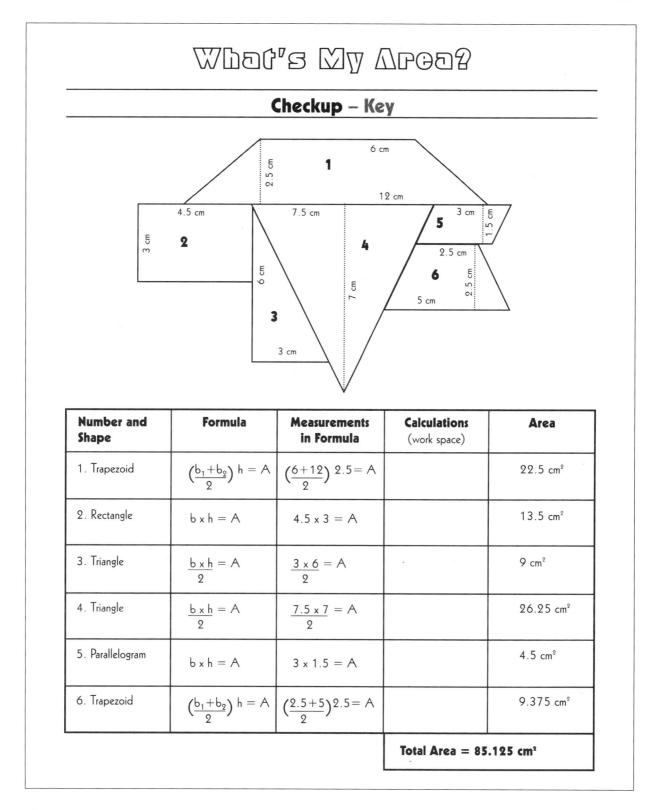

Number and Shape	Formula	Measurements in Formula	Calculations (work space)	Area
1. Trapezoid	$\left(\dfrac{b_1+b_2}{2}\right) h = A$	$\left(\dfrac{6+12}{2}\right) 2.5 = A$		22.5 cm²
2. Rectangle	$b \times h = A$	$4.5 \times 3 = A$		13.5 cm²
3. Triangle	$\dfrac{b \times h}{2} = A$	$\dfrac{3 \times 6}{2} = A$		9 cm²
4. Triangle	$\dfrac{b \times h}{2} = A$	$\dfrac{7.5 \times 7}{2} = A$		26.25 cm²
5. Parallelogram	$b \times h = A$	$3 \times 1.5 = A$		4.5 cm²
6. Trapezoid	$\left(\dfrac{b_1+b_2}{2}\right) h = A$	$\left(\dfrac{2.5+5}{2}\right) 2.5 = A$		9.375 cm²
			Total Area = 85.125 cm²	

Figure 4.14

5

Weighted Rubrics

THE PURPOSE OF WEIGHTED RUBRICS

Weighted rubrics are rubrics that give additional weight to concepts or performances thought to be more important to the task. This type of rubric uses multipliers to increase the value of specific criteria. When grading a piece of student work, it might become apparent that some criteria are more important than others, or some part of a performance is more crucial to understanding than another. When this is the case, a weighted rubric is of great value. For example, if the component *neatness* is important to the teacher, but not as important as the computational aspects of a task, a weighted rubric would be the solution. With a weighted rubric, students can easily see that some components are deemed more important than others and therefore know where to spend the majority of their time. Students respond well to the additional information that weighted rubrics provide. An example of a weighted rubric designed to evaluate a double bar graph or double line graph is provided in Figure 5.1.

The criteria listed in the left-hand column of the figure are important to the successful completion of the graph, but perhaps they do not hold equal importance to each other. In the far right-hand column, a weight or point value multiplier is listed for each criteria. The criteria with a higher multiplier are deemed more crucial to the understanding of the task in comparison to the others. When selecting the weight to be used for each category, teachers need to decide the importance of the criteria. Teachers should ask themselves: Is the category twice as important as others, five times as important, or more?

Criteria	0 Points	1 Point	2 Points	3 Points	
Graph title	Not present	Present	• Present • Appropriate to topic	• Present • Appropriate to topic • Correct capitalization and spelling	___ × 2 = ___
Axes titles	Not present	Present	• Present • Appropriate to topic	• Present • Appropriate to topic • Correct capitalization and spelling	___ × 2 = ___
Numbering/ Labeling x-axis	Inaccurate	Accurate	• Accurate • Well placed	• Accurate • Well placed • Easy to read	___ × 2 = ___
Numbering/ Labeling y-axis	Inaccurate	Accurate	• Accurate • Well placed	• Accurate • Well placed • Easy to read	___ × 2 = ___
Data	Incomplete	Inaccurately graphed	Accurately graphed	• Accurately graphed • Neat	___ × 10 = ___
Key	Not present	Inaccurate	Accurate	• Accurate • Neat	___ × 2 = ___
Overall Neatness	Sloppy	Room for improvement	Neat	Perfect!	___ × 1 = ___

Name _____ Evaluator _____ Points Possible = 63 Points Earned = _____

Grading Scale: 57 – 63 = A 50 – 56 = B 43 – 49 = C 37 – 42 = D 36 and below = F

Figure 5.1

When creating a weighted rubric, teachers need not try to predetermine the amount of total rubric points. Point values for rubrics can vary. A 100-point scale is not needed to use percent grades. Teachers can begin to develop the weighted rubric by establishing the number of levels and the corresponding point value, creating the rubric, and determining the desired weights.

When using this rubric to evaluate a product, the teacher determines the point value that most appropriately fits each level of performance. The teacher then uses the multipliers to determine the final score in each category. For example, if totally accurate computations are worth 4 points, and the multiplier is worth 5 points, this criterion would be worth 20 points on a project with perfect computations.

Individual scores for each criterion are added to reach the final rubric score. Teachers can calculate the total points possible by taking the highest point level on the rubric and multiplying that number by the sum of the multipliers. For example, the rubric in Figure 5.1 has a 4 as the highest level and its multipliers total 21. The total points possible on this rubric are calculated by multiplying 4 by 21, which equals 84 points. To determine a percent for a final rubric score, teachers should divide the points earned by the points possible and round to the nearest percent. It is important to remember that the percent calculated directly from the rubric might be low and might not fit into a traditional grading scale. Additional points may need to be added to create a fair grade. After all, a Level 2 performance on the rubric in Figure 5.1 is an adequate performance, which might indicate a grade of B or a C in a traditional grading system, but 2 out of 3 as a percent is only 66%. The chart in Figure 5.2 offers tips for turning the rubric percent into one that better fits a traditional grading system. (For more information on converting rubric scores to letter grades, see Appendix 2.)

Weighted rubrics are easy to create and useful when prioritizing criteria. To educators, the weighted rubric emphasizes quality in all areas of a product without sacrificing the opportunity to stress categories that might be more important to the mathematical understanding of the work.

If the Rubric Percent Is Equal To:	Grades
88–100	A
75–87	B
62–74	C
50–61	D
0–49	F

Figure 5.2

USING TECHNOLOGY IN RUBRIC DEVELOPMENT

There are many ways that technology can be used to aid in the rubric development process. Teachers can start by locating their district's benchmarks on their district's Web site. Once this has been done and the teacher has developed a checklist, he or she can use a spreadsheet program, such as Microsoft Word (using text boxes), Excel, or rubric-design software, such as the Rubricator, to set up the rubric.

Technology can also be helpful for collecting ideas for rubrics from educators and schools around the world. There are numerous Web sites devoted to rubrics; many offer rubrics that can be reproduced for classroom use. Typing the word *rubrics* in any of the major search engines (e.g., Google, Yahoo!, or HotBot) will yield a large variety of such sites. However, just because a rubric is on the Internet does not necessarily mean it is a quality rubric. Make sure to check rubrics for sensibility, clarity of descriptors, use of point values, applicability to standards, simplicity of language, and basic setup (e.g., easy to read and easy for students to understand).

The following rubric sites and rubric-related sites contain information on rubrics:

1. Rubrics for Web Lessons (http://edweb.sdsu.edu/webquest/rubrics/weblessons.htm): Contains links to articles about rubrics and authentic assessment, holistic rubrics for various topics, a rubric template, and other rubric resources.

2. Using Rubrics in Middle School (http://www.middleweb.com/rubricsHG.html): Features tips for creating rubrics and examples of analytic rubrics for such areas as book reports, oral presentations, persuasive essays, and more.

3. Evaluation Rubrics for Web Sites (http://www.siec.k12.in.us/~west/online/eval.htm): Includes rubrics that primary, intermediate, and secondary students can use to evaluate Web sites on the Internet when conducting Internet research.

4. Kathy Schrock's Guide for Educators—Assessment Rubrics (http://school.discovery.com/schrockguide/assess.html): Provides a categorized, annotated list of more than 1,600 sites to help educators, teachers, and parents enhance instruction and support the curriculum.

5. Kid Language Writing Rubrics (http://www.intercom.net/local/school/sdms/mspap/kidwrit.html): Contains analytic rubrics designed for middle school students for topics such as writing to inform, writing to persuade, and writing for personal expression.

6. Mother of All Rubrics (http://arc.missouri.edu/pa/olive.html): Includes an analytic rubric teachers can use to assess their rubric evaluation.

7. Evaluation Plan for Rubrics (http://volweb.utk.edu/Schools/bedford/harrisms/letterrubric.htm): Features analytic rubrics for friendly letters and business letters, as well as student samples of both.

RUBRIC/MATHEMATICS APPLICATION

DISCOVERIES IN RAINBOW CANDY LAND

In the following application, students change fractions to decimals and then to percents to determine the percentage of various colored candies in a package. This application contains a weighted rubric that can be used to assess the task. An overview of the application is provided in Figure 5.3.

Performance Task Explanation

This task helps students understand the relationship between fractions, decimals, and percentages. While completing the task, students are expected to manipulate numbers from one form to another. Through performance and discussion, students learn that different forms of numbers can be used in different ways. Decimals and percents, for example, are better than fractions when used to compare two numbers.

Task procedures are described in the overview and in Figure 5.4. To begin the process, students need a fun-size bag of colored candies (e.g., M&M's). Using the data collection chart (see Figure 5.5), students record several pieces of information. Students can also be encouraged to create a data chart of their own. A sample that shows how students can use the data collection chart is provided in Figure 5.6.

This performance task can typically be completed in three 45-minute class periods. If calculators and computers are used to make a chart and list data, the project should take middle school students approximately two 45-minute class periods. (Helpful hint: After giving the students the candy, have them open it and pour the contents into a clear zipper-type sandwich bag. When the bag is sealed, the students can manipulate the candy without being concerned about the condition of their desktop or the cleanliness of their hands.)

Figure 5.4   **Figure 5.5**   **Figure 5.6**

In the first column of the chart, students record the colors found in each package. Colors may not be the same for every student because every color is not in every bag.

The second column should list the exact number of colored candies found of each color. Students then determine the total number of candies in each bag and create fractions to express the amount of each color compared to the total amount of candy.

Unit Overview

Discoveries in Rainbow Candy Land

Standards:	Numbers and Operations, Data Analysis and Probability, Communication, Representation
Mathematics concepts:	Changing fractions to decimals to percents
Grade levels:	4 through 9
Related curricular areas:	Language arts—writing an explanation, writing a business letter
Materials:	One package of fun-size colored candies for each student or cooperative group
Task:	The Rainbow Candy Corporation has uncovered possible inconsistencies within their fun size packages of colored candies. Customers have been voicing their opinions about varying amounts of colors between packages. The research department is requesting your help. They need you to determine if the claims are accurate. They would also like a report of your findings.

Suggested Student Procedures

1. Find out how many candies there are of each color. Write each number as a fraction of the total and as a decimal and a percent.
2. Organize the information in an easy-to-understand chart.
3. Explain how you arrived at your mathematical answers.
4. Share your findings with the class. Discuss class discoveries.
5. Write a letter to the Rainbow Candy Corporation sharing class findings. Include observations and recommendations.

Teacher Resources

Task Explanation and Suggested Procedures page
Data Collection Chart and Sample Key
Explanations and Examples form and Sample Key
Rubric
Fractions, Decimals, and Percents Checkup and Key

Internet Resources

LightSpan: Provides mathematics study skills and tips, puzzles and problems, and links to articles and other Web sites. (http://www.lightspan.com)

SOS Math: This great study site for high school students provides mathematics review material ranging from algebra to differential equations. (http://www.sosmath.com)

Math League: This site offers information on mathematics contests for students in prekindergarten through high school, as well as sample contests and activities. (http://www.mathleague.com)

Figure 5.3

The numerator (top) of the fraction is the number specific to the color. The denominator (bottom) of the fraction is the total number of candies found in the package.

Next, students change the fractions into decimals and then into percents. To convert the fraction into a decimal, students divide the numerator by the denominator. To find the percent, students multiply the decimal by 100. (The percent can also be found by moving the decimal two places to the right.) Calculators are an option at this point of the task, but if the purpose is to practice skills in dividing decimals, teachers may want to make this a paper-and-pencil exercise. Upon completion of each section of the chart, students should explain, in writing, the procedure used to arrive at answers. The Explanations and Examples form (see Figure 5.7) can be used for this purpose. Figure 5.8, which was completed by a student, shows an example of how a student might fill out this form.

While students are completing calculations, teachers should encourage discussion. Remind students that they are fact finders on a research mission. You can ask students the following questions:

- What have you learned about the packages?
- Are your findings important to you?
- Do class discoveries support individual data?
- What conclusions can be drawn?
- What discoveries were made?
- What should be communicated to the company?

Business Letter

Review business letter format with students before they begin the letter-writing process. This portion of the task may be integrated into the language arts classroom and completed during that time.

Rubric

Rubrics should be discussed at the same time the task explanation is distributed. Students should have copies of both available to them throughout the task. The rubric used for this task is a 4-point weighted rubric (see Figure 5.9). The layout of this rubric is different from others in previous chapters. This rubric is set up vertically, and levels of performance are listed beneath each other. The highest level of performance for each criterion is listed at the top of the section. Share all of the 4-point descriptors with students and point out the weights accompanying each section of the rubric.

When evaluating student performance, choose the descriptor for each criterion that best describes the product or performance. Each descriptor has a point value, and each section has a numerical weight. To calculate the value for each category, multiply the point

Figure 5.7

Figure 5.8

Figure 5.9

Figure 5.10a   **Figure 5.10b**   **Figure 5.11a**   **Figure 5.11b**

value earned by the weight. When evaluation is complete, add all individual calculations to obtain the total rubric score.

Expanding the Task

Graphing the results extends the performance task. Students can create a bar graph to record their data. A separate bar for each candy color will assist students in the comparisons they make. Creating a class or cooperative-group multiple-line graph also makes an interesting visual.

Simplifying the Task

The performance task can be simplified for younger students. To simplify, provide every student the same number of candies; 25 works well. If there are more than 25 candies in the package, students are usually happy to eat a few. If there are fewer, hand out extras so each student has a total of 25. Students can concentrate on creating fractions representative of each color. Fractions can be compared throughout the class because the denominators will be the same. Decimals and fractions can be calculated as a class project. Calculators can help simplify this process.

Checkup

The assessment provided in the checkup (see Figure 5.10) is a traditional form of a teacher-made assessment. It can be used before or after the task. An answer key for the assessment is provided in Figure 5.11. Prior to the task, use the checkup to determine the current knowledge level of students. Then make instructional decisions regarding student readiness for the task. If used after completing the task, student performance will demonstrate the students' depth of understanding.

When tasks are completed, displaying student work adds to students' sense of accomplishment. Encourage students to explain their projects and findings to other students. This will increase their level of understanding.

IN SUMMARY

When students are interested in their work, they learn more and retain information longer. The task provided in this chapter will interest students and give them opportunities to practice skills and explain thinking. The task assists students in seeing the relationships among fractions, decimals, and percents.

The weighted rubric provides clear expectations and gives students a target. In this task, the skills of calculating fractions, decimals, and percents and explaining procedures are worth more than some of the other skills of the task; therefore, a weighted rubric is used. Teachers can experiment with point values when they create rubrics that require varied point values.

Discoveries in Rainbow Candy Land

Task Explanation and Suggested Procedures

Task:

The Rainbow Candy Corporation has uncovered possible inconsistencies within their fun size packages of colored candies. Customers have been voicing their opinions about varying amounts of colors between packages. The research department is requesting your help. They need you to determine if the claims are accurate. They would also like a report of your findings.

Suggested Procedures:

1. Find out how many candies there are of each color. Write each number as a fraction of the total and as a decimal and a percent.

2. Organize the information in an easy-to-understand chart.

3. Explain how you arrived at your mathematical answers.

4. Share your findings with the class. Discuss class discoveries.

5. Write a letter to the Rainbow Candy Corporation sharing class findings. Include observations and recommendations.

Figure 5.4

Discoveries in Rainbow Candy Land

Data Collection Chart

Use this graphic organizer to record the candy color information and the fractions, decimals, and percents.

Procedures:

1. In the first column, write the names of all of the colors found in your package of candy.

2. In the second column, write the number of candies you have of each color.

3. In the third column, write the fraction for each color. The numerator is the number of candy in the specific color; the denominator is the total number of candies in the package.

4. In the fourth column, record the decimals that correspond to each fraction. To calculate the decimal, divide the numerator of each fraction by its denominator.

5. In the last column, write each number as a percent of the total. To change the decimal to a percent, multiply by 100 (or move the decimal two places to the right).

Colors	Number of Candies per Color	Number as Fraction	Number as Decimal	Number as Percent
Totals				

Figure 5.5

Discoveries in Rainbow Candy Land

Data Collection Chart—Sample Key

Use this graphic organizer to record the candy color information and the fractions, decimals, and percents.

Procedures:

1. In the first column, write the names of all of the colors found in your package of candy.

2. In the second column, write the number of candies you have of each color.

3. In the third column, write the fraction for each color. The numerator is the number of candy in the specific color; the denominator is the total number of candies in the package.

4. In the fourth column, record the decimals that correspond to each fraction. To calculate the decimal, divide the numerator of each fraction by its denominator.

5. In the last column, write each number as a percent of the total. To change the decimal to a percent, multiply by 100 (or move the decimal two places to the right).

Colors	Number of Candies per Color	Number as Fraction	Number as Decimal	Number as Percent
orange	5	5/25 = 1/5	0.2	20%
green	6	6/25	0.24	24%
blue	7	7/25	0.28	28%
red	2	2/25	0.08	8%
yellow	5	5/25 = 1/5	0.2	20%
Totals	25	25/25	1.00	100%

Figure 5.6

Discoveries in Rainbow Candy Land

Explanations and Examples

Answer questions in complete sentences.

1. How did you create the fractions on your chart?

2. How did you change the fractions into decimals? Include an example.

3. How did you change the decimals to percents? Include an example.

4. What discoveries did you make about your data?

Figure 5.7

Discoveries in Rainbow Candy Land

Explanations and Examples—Sample Answers

Answer questions in complete sentences.

1. How did you create the fractions on your chart?
   I put the number from the color over the total number candies.

2. How did you change the fractions into decimals? Include an example.
   I divided the numerator by the denominator.
   2/25 would be 2 ÷ 25.

3. How did you change the decimals to percents? Include an example.
   I multiplied the decimal by 100.
   .08 × 100 = 8%

4. What discoveries did you make about your data?
   I found out that my data was different from what other kids found in their packages.

Figure 5.8

Discoveries in Rainbow Candy Land
Rubric

Instructions: Circle or highlight the appropriate point values. Multiply each by the weight of the category. Add all points together.

Performance			Value x Weight = Total
Chart	Chart is complete, neat, and easy to read	4	
	Chart is neat and easy to read, 1 item missing	3	x 2 = _____
	Chart is neat and easy to read, 2 items missing	2	
	Chart is messy or 3 or more items are missing	1	
Fractions	All fractions are present and accurate	4	
	1 fraction is incorrect or not present	3	x 5 = _____
	2 fractions are incorrect or not present	2	
	3 or more fractions are incorrect or not present	1	
Decimals	All decimals are present and accurate	4	
	1 decimal is incorrect or not present	3	x 5 = _____
	2 decimals are incorrect or not present	2	
	3 or more decimals are incorrect or not present	1	
Percents	All percents are present and accurate	4	
	1 percent is incorrect or not present	3	x 5 = _____
	2 percents are incorrect or not present	2	
	3 or more percents are incorrect	1	
Explanations	Explanations present for fractions, decimals, and percents Well-written and easy to understand Examples are included Grammar and spelling are perfect	4	
	Explanations present for fractions, decimals, and percents Well written and easy to understand Grammar and spelling are perfect	3	x 10 = _____
	Explanations present for fractions, decimals, and percents confusing OR 1–3 grammar and spelling errors	2	
	Explanations have portions missing OR confusing OR 4 or more grammar and spelling errors	1	
Letter	Form includes correct heading, inside address, greeting, body, closing, and signature Well written, neat, and easy to understand All punctuation, grammar, and spelling is accurate	4	
	Form includes correct heading, inside address, greeting, body, closing, and signature Well written, neat, and easy to understand 1–2 errors in punctuation, grammar, or spelling	3	x 3 = _____
	Form includes correct heading, inside address, greeting, body, closing, and signature Well written, neat, and easy to understand 3–4 errors in punctuation, grammar, or spelling	2	
	Proper form not used OR 5 or more errors in punctuation, grammar, or spelling	1	

Evaluator: _____   Points Possible = 120   Points Earned = _____

Figure 5.9

Discoveries in Rainbow Candy Land

Fractions, Decimals, and Percents Checkup
Page 1

Name: _____   Points earned: _____ /40   Grade: _____

Circle the letter of the correct answer. (1 point each)

1. $1/4 =$
   a) 0.14   b) 0.25   c) 0.4   d) 2.5

2. $3/5 =$
   a) 1.67   b) 0.35   c) 0.6   d) 3.5

3. $2\frac{3}{4} =$
   a) 2.75   b) 2.34   c) 2.133   d) 27.5

4. $5\frac{3}{8} =$
   a) 53.75   b) 5.375   c) 537.5   d) 5.267

5. $5.67 =$
   a) 0.0567%   b) 0.567%   c) 56.7%   d) 567%

6. $0.45 =$
   a) 45%   b) 4.5%   c) 0.0045%   d) 0.045%

7. $62\% =$
   a) 6.2   b) 0.62   c) 6,200   d) 620.0

8. $358\% =$
   a) 35.8   b) 3.58   c) 358   d) 3,580

9. $3/12 =$
   a) 312%   b) 4%   c) 25%   d) 40%

10. $3/10 =$
    a) 30%   b) 310%   c) 33.3%   d) 0.3%

Fill in the blank with the correct response. (3 points each)

11. The top number of a fraction is called a _____.

12. The bottom number of a fraction is called a _____.

13. The % sign represents the word _____.

14. When changing a decimal to a percent, the decimal point moves to the _____.

Write a short answer. (3 points each)

15. How do you change a fraction to a decimal?

_____

_____

_____

_____

Figure 5.10   (Continued)

Discoveries in Rainbow Candy Land

Fractions, Decimals, and Percents Checkup   Page 2

16. Mrs. Etser spends about $3.00 out of every $8.00 of her money on food for her family. What percent of money does she spend on food? Explain your answer.

_____

_____

_____

17. 85% of Mr. Ducken's class wore red during Red Ribbon Week. 7 out of every 8 of Mrs. Crosbert's students wore red. Which class had the higher percentage of students wearing red? Explain your answer.

_____

_____

_____

18. Mrs. Mortler, the principal, said that if the student body could raise 75% of the cost of a new playground, the school could afford the rest. The playground cost is $30,000. The students raised $23,000. Was that enough money to get the playground? Explain your answer.

_____

_____

_____

19. Mrs. Klima, the manager of a local toy store, conducted a study to see how many of her customers were children. She found that from 10:00 a.m. until 2:00 p.m. 6 out of every 8 customers were children. Between the hours of 2:00 p.m. and 6:00 p.m., 9 out of every 15 customers were children. During which hours are there a higher percentage of children in the store? What are the percents?

_____

_____

_____

20. Mrs. Brecker plants a variety of flowers in her garden. She is interested in keeping track of the percent of each type of flower she plants this year. Her garden consists of 17 geraniums, 13 begonias, 9 mums, and 11 zinnias. What percentage of her garden is made up of each type of flower?

_____

_____

_____

Figure 5.10

Discoveries in Rainbow Candy Land

Fractions, Decimals, and Percents Checkup – Key   Page 1

Name:_____   Points earned:_____/50   Grade:_____

Circle the letter of the correct answer. (1 point each)

1. 1/4 =
   a) 0.14   **b) 0.25**   c) 0.4   d) 2.5

2. 3/5 =
   a) 1.67   b) 0.35   **c) 0.6**   d) 3.5

3. $2^3/_4$ =
   a) 2.75   b) 2.34   c) 2.133   d) 27.5

4. $5^3/_8$ =
   a) 53.75   **b) 5.375**   c) 537.5   d) 5.267

5. 5.67 =
   a) 0.0567%   b) 0.567%   c) 56.7%   **d) 567%**

6. 0.45 =
   a) 45%   b) 4.5%   c) 0.0045%   d) 0.045%

7. 62% =
   a) 6.2   **b) 0.62**   c) 6200   d) 620.0

8. 358% =
   a) 35.8   **b) 3.58**   c) 358   d) 3580

9. 3/12 =
   a) 312%   b) 4%   **c) 25%**   d) 40%

10. 3/10 =
    a) 30%   b) 310%   c) 33.3%   d) 0.3%

Fill in the blank with the correct response. (3 points each)

11. The top number of a fraction is called a ___numerator___.

12. The bottom number of a fraction is called a ___denominator___.

13. The % sign represents the word ___percent___.

14. When changing a decimal to a percent, the decimal point moves to the ___right___.

Write a short answer. (3 points)

15. How do you change a fraction to a decimal? ___Divide the numerator by the denominator.___

Figure 5.11   (Continued)

Discoveries in Rainbow Candy Land

Fractions, Decimals, and Percents Checkup – Key   Page 2

16. Mrs. Etser spends about $3.00 out of every $8.00 of her money on food for her family. What percent of money does she spend on food? Explain your answer.

    3/8 of her money is equal to 37.5%. That means she spends 37.5% of her money on food.

17. 85% of Mr. Ducken's class wore red during Red Ribbon Week. 7 out of every 8 of Mrs. Crosbert's students wore red. Which class had the higher percentage of students wearing red? Explain your answer.

    7 out of 8 students is equal to 87.5% so Mrs. Crosbert had more students wearing red.

18. Mrs. Mortler, the principal, said that if the student body could raise 75% of the cost of a new playground, the school could afford the rest. The playground cost is $30,000. The students raised $23,000. Was that enough money to get the playground? Explain your answer.

    23000/30000 is equal to about 77% so the students did raise enough money.

19. Mrs. Klima, the manager of a local toy store, did a study to see how many of her customers were children. She found that from 10:00 a.m. until 2:00 p.m. 6 out of every 8 customers were children. Between the hours of 2:00 p.m. and 6:00 p.m., 9 out of every 15 customers were children. During which hours are there a higher percent of children in the store? What are the percents?

    More children were in the store between 10:00 and 2:00. 75% were children.

    Between 2:00 and 6:00 only 60% were children.

20. Mrs. Brecker plants a variety of flowers in her garden. She is interested in keeping track of the percent of each type of flower she plants this year. Her garden consists of 17 geraniums, 13 begonias, 9 mums, and 11 zinnias. What percent of her garden is made up of each type of flower?

    Geraniums = 34%   Begonias = 26%

    Mums = 18%   Zinnias = 22%

Figure 5.11

6

Student-Created Rubrics

USING STUDENT-CREATED RUBRICS

Students, as well as everyone else, appreciate having input into things that affect their lives. When students are being evaluated on a product or performance, they may feel it is crucial that their input be part of the process. When this input occurs, students gain a deeper understanding of the task they are performing. They not only come to understand what is expected of them, but also they begin to feel ownership in the process because they contributed to the expectations.

For students to learn best, mathematics must be made meaningful to them, and students must be shown the purpose of their studies in a real-world setting. Therefore, performance tasks and problems should be based on mathematics applications—tasks that apply mathematics in settings beyond the textbook and actively involve the student. Such mathematics applications must be evaluated with task-specific rubrics that allow students to solve problems they might find in everyday life. For example, using mathematics to figure out a monthly budget or to determine the best deal on a car loan are both examples of real-world mathematics applications. With some initial teacher direction, students can become experts at helping to create rubrics.

To develop rubrics, students require guidance for the performance task focus and essential knowledge. Teachers can help students discern task focus by asking them what is expected of them on completion of a task, what they should know and be able to do, and what the evidence will look like. Students are often adept at understanding the purpose of a task and can normally list the criteria fairly well. However, if students miss something crucial to the understanding, the teacher should be prepared to ask students to add that component. With practice, students will be able to pinpoint important criteria and describe what a high level of performance looks like for those criteria, as well as provide insight into mathematical quality performance descriptors. According to Protheroe, Shellard, and Turner (2004), for students to do well on assignments they must clearly understand the expectations. Student-created rubrics are the perfect tool to achieve that end.

There are many benefits when students aid in rubric development. Developing rubrics helps students clearly understand the task, the expectations, and the evaluation process. Students take pride in their performance and ownership in the entire process (Ainsworth & Christinson, 1998). Students have much to contribute to a rubric and are more motivated to produce high-quality work when they are involved in the process, and teachers often find that the quality of the students' products often increases noticeably when they use student-generated rubrics (Danielson, 1997).

To fully support student-created rubrics, teachers must recognize how important it is for students to take responsibility for their learning. It is crucial that students understand the reasons material is being presented to them as well as the part they play in the development of that knowledge. Through the rubric development process, students begin to understand the importance of assessment criteria. They gain a deeper comprehension into the purpose and the depth of their own understanding. Providing students with the opportunity to pinpoint the knowledge essential to understanding a concept gives them experience with thinking critically about what is important in the demonstration of knowledge. As a result, students become aware of what they need to know and at what level they need to perform for a successful experience.

In addition, when students contribute to a rubric, they typically find themselves more accountable to the standards. They internalize the standards and gain an in-depth comprehension of concepts. As a result of the discussion, students understand the role standards play in rubric development and, thus, project success. The rubric has the capability of providing focus and inspiring motivation (Rose, 1999); in this way, the rubric not only acts as an assessment tool for students but becomes a learning tool as well.

THE PROCESS

A teacher can start the student rubric development process by focusing on the task standards. The task-standards link is crucial when developing and evaluating a real-life application. The teacher needs to make sure that successful completion of the task shows that students have grasped the knowledge essential to the standards. When the teacher is certain that the task relates to the standards and the details of the performance have been outlined, he or she should share the task with the students. The teacher must clearly explain the task to help students create the evaluation rubric. To provide valuable input, students need to understand the task and its intended purpose. The teacher can also discuss the standards and benchmarks with students to help them develop criteria for the rubric.

Next, the teacher should distribute a blank rubric to the students (see Figure 6.1) and request their suggestions for what is important for successful completion of the task. The think-write-pair-share strategy is a good tool to use during this time (see Figure 6.2). The teacher can allow students 2 minutes of brainstorming time to generate some appropriate criteria, ask students to spend another 1 or 2 minutes writing the criteria on the back of their blank rubric, and then give them 2 minutes to share their criteria with a partner and add more ideas to their own lists.

The next step is to create a list of criteria with the class. Teachers can solicit responses from as many pairs as necessary until all ideas have been shared and the list has been generated. At this point, any essential criteria that are not currently on the list should be added by prompting students. To generate additional responses, ask students questions such as the following: Do you think we might add . . . ? How will we evaluate . . . ? Have we covered this standard?

At this point, the list needs to be grouped, combined, and pared down. Similar criteria should be grouped, and criteria that are alike should be combined. The teachers should discuss with students any criteria that might not apply or would not be possible to evaluate and eliminate them. It is important that the final criteria accurately measure the performance. Five to 10 criteria are reasonable.

Students can list the criteria on their rubrics and begin developing descriptors in cooperative groups or as a class. Students should concentrate on the Level 4 performance first. The teacher should stress to students that descriptors must be specific and that students should ask themselves what an exemplary level of accomplishment looks like and describe that. The teacher can encourage students to be realistic but to set high expectations. If the task is one that has been completed by a previous group of students, the teacher can show examples of the finished performances to help students visualize and describe top levels of quality. When this process is used regularly, students become experts in the development process.

Student input can end at this point. The impact of the rubric on student performance results from students taking ownership of the criteria and the descriptors at the highest level of quality. To save time, the teacher can complete Levels 1 through 3 without further student input and present them to the class.

Teachers can then create the master rubric using student-generated criteria and descriptors for Level 4. This can be done by collecting the descriptors and summarizing them when making the final rubric. After the rubric is complete, the teacher should discuss all of the criteria and descriptors with students and distribute the final rubric before they begin the task.

A summary of these steps is provided in Figure 6.3.

Student-Generated Rubric

Task: _____

Criteria	Levels of Quality—Descriptors			
	1	2	3	4

Figure 6.1

Think-Write-Pair-Share

THINK—Spend 2 minutes thinking of criteria or evidence that is crucial to the completion of the task.

WRITE—Spend 1 to 2 minutes writing a list of points from the Think step.

PAIR—Quickly choose a partner.

SHARE—Spend 2 minutes sharing your list with your partner. Add your partner's ideas to your list.

Figure 6.2

Steps for Creating Student-Generated Rubrics

1. The teacher develops a performance task based on standards and benchmarks.
2. The teacher describes the performance task and its purpose to students.
3. Students develop evaluation criteria.
4. Students create descriptors for Level 4.
5. The teacher creates descriptors for Levels 1–3.
6. The teacher completes and distributes the rubric.

Figure 6.3

Evaluating student understanding and performance can be an enlightening experience for both students and teachers when students take an active part in the assessment process. Student-created rubrics result in products that exhibit increased levels of quality and students who demonstrate a new level of pride in their accomplishments.

RUBRIC/MATHEMATICS APPLICATION

I'M NOT JUST AVERAGE!

In the following application, students calculate mean, median, mode, and range. The rubric provided for this application was developed with students. Teachers can use this rubric or create a rubric with their students. The task overview (see Figure 6.4) outlines the basic information about the task.

Performance Task Explanation

Many students are involved in sports both within and outside of school. Sports statistics are kept for every facet of professional athletics, and many are recorded for recreational programs as well. Students are aware of batting averages, free throw percentages, percentage of pass completions, average number of assists per game, bowling averages, average number of yards per drive, and hundreds more statistics for every sport imaginable. One of the many purposes of this task is to have students calculate statistics. Another is to have students use statistical information to form an opinion about a team and its season. This task takes approximately four 45-minute class periods.

Any sport can be the subject of this task. Football was chosen because there are fewer games per season than the majority of other professional sports, which makes calculations

Figure 6.5

easier for students. Some students may need assistance picking a team to use for the task. The teams in the National Football League (NFL) are listed in Figure 6.5, and this information can be copied and passed out to students.

Figure 6.6   **Figure 6.7**   **Figure 6.8**

A team's previous season's scores and opponents are listed on the team's Web site. This information also can be researched through the NFL at www.nfl.com. Students can print out the information or copy it onto their record chart. Figure 6.6 outlines the problem and procedures for students.

Following the gathering of data using the Data Collection Chart (see Figure 6.7), students can create a graphic organizer to record the mean, median, mode, and range for the scores the team achieved. The graphic organizer included in Figure 6.8 could also be used for this purpose. Students should also find the mean, median, mode, and range of the combined opponents' scores.

If the teacher's goal for this assignment includes reviewing whole number and decimal operations, students may be asked to show all calculations. If finding statistical information is the only goal, students can use calculators.

Students should describe the methods used to find the mean, median, mode, and range. The numbers and equations should be included in their explanations. When calculations are complete, students can place results in the proper location on the graphic organizer.

Reflections

Once students have gathered their statistics, they need to take time to analyze the results. Probing questions might help students look at data more deeply. Teachers can ask students the following questions:

- Which average makes your team look the best: mean, median, or mode?
- Which average would typically be reported?
- What can you conclude about the season by looking at the range?
- Could the mean of the choice team versus the mean of the opponent's team indicate a winning or losing season?
- Why do teams keep statistics?

Figure 6.9

Unit Overview

I'm Not Just Average!

Standards:	Numbers and Operations, Data Analysis and Probability, Problem Solving, Communication, Connections
Mathematics concepts:	Calculating mean, median, mode, and range
Grade levels:	4 through 9
Related curricular areas:	Language arts—Writing an explanation; Technology—Using the Internet
Materials:	Computer with Internet access
Task:	The National Football League (NFL) is experiencing a glitch in its new statistical software. Comparisons need to be made between teams and the previous season's scores, but the computers have malfunctioned. Without this information, record books cannot be filled out. The NFL needs your help in finding the statistics necessary to make the comparisons.

Suggested Student Procedures

1. Choose your favorite NFL team. Using the Internet, find the final scores from all of the previous season's games. Try the team's Web site or go to www.nfl.com.

2. Create a chart to record all of the scores in chronological order from the first to the last game. Include the opponents' team names on the chart.

3. Find the mean, median, mode, and range of all of the scores achieved by your team.

4. Find the mean, median, mode, and range of the combined opponents' scores.

5. Write a paragraph describing your team's season. Include comparisons among the mean, median, and mode. Express your opinions.

6. Organize the information into a booklet. Include explanations of the processes used to find the mean, median, mode, and range.

Teacher Resources

Teams in the NFL page

Task Explanation and Suggested Procedure page

Data Collection Chart

Explanations and Statistics Organizer

Checklist

Rubric

Measure of Central Tendency Checkup and Key

Internet Resources

All Math: Offers tools and activities for students, including a mathematics glossary, metric conversion tools, flash cards, games, and links to other mathematics sites. (http://www.allmath.com)

Mudd Math Fun Facts: Features fun facts for areas of mathematics study from geometry to calculus for teachers to use in classroom discussion. (http://www.math.hmc.edu/funfacts)

Algebra Help: Helps students with algebra questions by offering lesson summaries, a calculator that takes students through the steps of solving the problem, and interactive worksheets. (http://www.algebrahelp.com)

Figure 6.4

After group discussion and comparison of results, students should write a personal reaction to their team's season. The statistical information they discover should be used in their reflections.

Checklist

The checklist in Figure 6.9 provides a simple reminder for students and can be posted in the room or distributed the day before the task is to be completed. By comparing what they have completed to the task components listed in the checklist, students will become aware of the steps needed to complete the performance task.

Figure 6.10

Rubric

The left side of the student-created rubric (see Figure 6.10) lists the components the students deemed to be important. The 3-point column describes the level of quality that students felt would illustrate a quality product. Although this is a 4-column rubric, its top value is only 3 points because students wanted the first column to be worth 0. The students made this decision because they felt that if a portion of the project were missing its creator should not be rewarded by accumulating points for work not attempted. For this task, students helped develop criteria for Levels 1 to 3 in addition to criteria for the Level 4 performance because they had experience in rubric development and wanted to extend their input into the rubric development process.

The day the project is due, students should peer-evaluate the projects by completing the rubric. This task should be taken seriously because the goal is for students to help each other see the strengths and weaknesses of their projects. Students should then be allowed to improve their performance before the final grade is given. Extending the due date by a day or two increases the level of quality exhibited in the products. The goal of any performance is to have students achieve at the highest level possible. If extending a deadline by a short amount of time does that, the extension is well worth it.

Expanding the Task

The performance task can be expanded by assigning different teams to students so that each student is responsible for a different team's statistics. Instead of writing reflections, students can write newspaper articles or editorials describing the team's season. These works, combined with season results and statistics, can be compiled and placed in an NFL informational booklet created by the class. Each chapter can highlight a different team, and students can create a chapter cover with team logos and names of players. They can even research the history of the team and insert additional information into their chapters. The completed booklet can be copied and distributed to school libraries within the district. Parents might also appreciate a copy.

Simplifying the Task

Students can be allowed to use calculators to complete all mathematical operations. This gives them the opportunity to work with statistics without being restricted by their ability to calculate.

Figure 6.11a   **Figure 6.11b**   **Figure 6.12a**   **Figure 6.12b**

To simplify the task for younger students, the teacher can concentrate on the mean and eliminate the median and the mode. The mean is the most common statistical average and students will benefit from understanding its use.

If teachers want to leave the task as is, but still simplify it, cooperative groups are a good option. Group members can work together to aid each other in comprehension and task completion.

Checkup

The Measure of Central Tendency assessment in Figure 6.11 is a combination of multiple choice, matching, and short-answer questions. The assessment gives students several opportunities to illustrate their knowledge of mean, median, mode, and range. The assessment can be used as a follow-up to the task or as an opportunity for practice before the task instead of a test. A key for the test is provided in Figure 6.12.

IN SUMMARY

Student-created rubrics are powerful tools because getting students involved in the evaluation process motivates them to succeed. Students are more likely to understand expectations and strive to perform at their highest levels of ability when they take part in creating the evaluation tool. They are also more likely to see the evaluation tool as a fair measure of abilities when they are given a chance to provide their input. In this way, student-created rubrics drive student performance.

I'm Not Just Average!

Teams in the NFL

National Football League

American Football Conference

Baltimore Ravens

Buffalo Bills

Cincinnati Bengals

Cleveland Browns

Denver Broncos

Indianapolis Colts

Jacksonville Jaguars

Kansas City Chiefs

Miami Dolphins

New England Patriots

New York Jets

Oakland Raiders

Pittsburgh Steelers

San Diego Chargers

Seattle Seahawks

Tennessee Titans

National Football Conference

Arizona Cardinals

Atlanta Falcons

Carolina Panthers

Chicago Bears

Dallas Cowboys

Detroit Lions

Green Bay Packers

Minnesota Vikings

New Orleans Saints

New York Giants

Philadelphia Eagles

St. Louis Rams

San Francisco 49ers

Tampa Bay Buccaneers

Washington Redskins

Figure 6.5

I'm Not Just Average!

Task Explanation and Suggested Procedures

Task:

The National Football League (NFL) is experiencing a glitch in its new statistical software. Comparisons need to be made between teams and the previous season's scores, but the computers have malfunctioned. Without this information, record books cannot be filled out. The NFL needs your help in finding the statistics necessary to make the comparisons.

Suggested Procedures:

1. Choose your favorite NFL team. Using the Internet, find the final scores from all the previous season's games. Try the team's Web site or go to www.nfl.com.

2. Create a chart to record all of the scores in chronological order from the first to the last game. Include the opponents' team names on the chart.

3. Find the mean, median, mode, and range of all the scores achieved by your team.

4. Find the mean, median, mode, and range of the combined opponents' scores.

5. Write a paragraph describing your team's season. Include comparisons among the mean, median, and mode. Express your opinions.

6. Organize the information into a booklet. Include explanations of the processes used to find the mean, median, mode, and range.

Figure 6.6

I'm Not Just Average!

Data Collection Chart

	Team Name and Season Year		
Game Number	**My Team's Score**	**Opponent's Score**	**Opponent's Name**
1			
2			
3			
4			
5			
6			
7			
8			
9			
10			
11			
12			
13			
14			
15			
16			

Figure 6.7

I'm Not Just Average!

Explanations and Statistics Organizer

Finding the Mean

Explanation:

Finding the Median

Explanation:

Finding the Mode

Explanation:

Finding the Range

Explanation:

Teams	Mean	Median	Mode	Range
Your Team's Scores				
Opponents' Combined Scores				

Figure 6.8

I'm Not Just Average!

Checklist

Do you have . . .	Yes!	Not yet.
A data chart of all previous season's scores for your team?		
An explanation of how to find the mean?		
The mean of your team and the opponents' combined mean?		
An explanation of how to find the median?		
The median of your team and the opponents' combined median?		
An explanation of how to find the mode?		
The mode of your team and the opponents' combined mode?		
An explanation of how to find the range?		
The range of your team and the opponents' combined range?		
A paragraph indicating your opinions comparing the season and the statistics you found?		
Correct spelling?		
A neat and attractive booklet?		
Your name on the booklet?		

Figure 6.9

I'm Not Just Average!

Rubric

Instructions: Highlight the area for each category that best describes the performance. Add points together to determine rubric score.

	0	**1**	**2**	**3**
Data Chart	Not present	Incomplete	Complete, lacks neatness	Complete, neat
Mean Your team	Not present	Mean or procedure inaccurate	Mean correct, procedure incomplete	Mean correct, procedure well illustrated
Opposing team	Not present	Mean or procedure inaccurate	Mean correct, procedure needs clarification	Mean correct, procedure well illustrated
Explanation	Not present or incorrect	Unclear	Correct with spelling errors	Well thought out, clear explanation
Median Your team	Not present	Median or procedure inaccurate	Median correct, procedure incomplete	Median correct, procedure well illustrated
Opposing team	Not present	Median or procedure inaccurate	Median correct, procedure needs clarification	Median correct, procedure well illustrated
Explanation	Not present or incorrect	Unclear	Correct with spelling errors	Well thought out, clear explanation
Mode Your team	Not present	Mode or procedure inaccurate	Mode correct, procedure incomplete	Mode correct, procedure well illustrated
Opposing team	Not present	Mode or procedure inaccurate	Mode correct, procedure needs clarification	Mode correct, procedure well illustrated
Explanation	Not present or incorrect	Unclear	Correct with spelling errors	Well thought out, clear explanation
Range Your team	Not present	Range or procedure inaccurate	Range correct, procedure incomplete	Range correct, procedure well illustrated
Opposing team	Not present	Range or procedure inaccurate	Range correct, procedure needs clarification	Range correct, procedure well illustrated
Explanation	Not present or incorrect	Unclear	Correct with spelling errors	Well thought out, well illustrated
Booklet	Not present or largely incomplete	Disorganized, information missing	Complete, organized	Complete, organized, attractive

Points possible = 42   Points earned =

Figure 6.10

I'm Not Just Average!

Measure of Central Tendency Checkup   Page 1

Name_____   Date_____

Choose the letter of the correct answer. Show all work. (2 points each)

1. James received the following scores while bowling: 126, 145, 165, 98, and 106. What is the mean?
    a.) 126   b.) 128   c.) 67   d.) no mean

2. Jamie is a waitress. On Monday she received $32 in tips, on Tuesday $27, on Wednesday $17, on Thursday $0, and on Friday $56. What is the average (mean) amount of tips received?
    a.) $27.00   b.) $27.40   c.) $33.00   d.) $26.40

3. Sheena received the following grades in mathematics: 100, 88, 88, 96, 78, 90. What is the median of these scores?
    a.) 90   b.) 88   c.) 89   d.) 91

4. Wassim sells used cars. In February he sold cars for $1,234, $2,678, $456, and $3,978. To the nearest cent, what is the mean price of these cars?
    a.) $1,669.20   b.) $1,956.00   c.) $2,086.50   d.) $2,006.25

Write the letter of the correct answer on the line. Show all calculations. (2 points each)
Use the following data points to complete the matching exercises: 128, 42, 78, 123, 1,234, 42, 156, 42, 156, 42, 692

_____ 5. mode

_____ 6. median

_____ 7. range

_____ 8. mean

a. 1,234

b. 1,192

c. 128 and 42

d. 123

e. 42

f. 248.63

g. 252

Figure 6.11   (Continued)

I'm Not Just Average!

Measure of Central Tendency Checkup   Page 2

Name_____   Date_____

Find answers for each problem. (20 points each)

9. The Green Bay Packers scored the following points in their first seven games: 27, 42, 0, 13, 21, 27, and 10. Find the mean, median, mode, and range.

   _____

   _____

10. Marissa got a new job. The first week she earned $130.25. The second week she earned $245.25. The third week she earned $238.75. This week she earned $312.75. Find the mean, median, mode, and range.

    _____

    _____

11. Andy wants his average bowling score to be no less than 120. The first game he bowled a 98. The second game he got 110. What is the lowest score he can get on the third game to have at least a 120 average?

    _____

    _____

12. Maria scored an average of 22 points in the first seven games of the basketball season. These are the scores for the first six games: 15, 18, 30, 12, 22, and 18. How many points did she score during the seventh game?

    _____

    _____

13. Rosie hopes to sell an average of at least $980 of merchandise each day in her store this week. On Sunday she took in $820, on Monday $675, on Tuesday $1,200, on Wednesday $1,000, on Thursday $726, and on Friday $1,300. What is the least amount of money she needs to take in on Saturday to reach her goal?

    _____

    _____

14. You received these five grade in mathematics: 88, 100, 88, 92, and 64. What is the mean, median, and mode of your grades?

    _____

    _____

Figure 6.11

I'm Not Just Average!

Measures of Central Tendency Checkup – Key   Page 1

Name_____   Date_____

Choose the letter of the correct answer. Show all work. (2 points each)

1. James received the following scores while bowling: 126, 145, 165, 98, and 106. What is the mean?
   a.) 126   (b.) 128)   c.) 67   d.) no mean

2. Jamie is a waitress. On Monday she received $32 in tips, on Tuesday $27, on Wednesday $17, on Thursday $0, and on Friday $56. What is the average (mean) amount of tips received?
   a.) $27.00   b.) $27.40   c.) $33.00   (d.) $26.40)

3. Sheena received the following grades in mathematics: 100, 88, 88, 96, 78, 90. What is the median of these scores?
   a.) 90   b.) 88   (c.) 89)   d.) 91

4. Wassim sells used cars. In February he sold cars for $1,234, $2,678, $456, and $3,978. To the nearest cent, what is the mean price of these cars?
   a.) $1,669.20   b.) $1,956.00   (c.) $2,086.50)   d.) $2,006.25

Write the letter of the correct answer on the line. Show all calculations. (2 points each)
Use the following data points to complete the matching exercises: 128, 42, 78, 123, 1,234, 42, 156, 42, 156, 42, 692

_e_ 5. mode	a.	1,234
_d_ 6. median	b.	1,192
_b_ 7. range	c.	128 and 42
_f_ 8. mean	d.	123
	e.	42
	f.	248.63
	g.	252

Figure 6.12   *(Continued)*

I'm Not Just Average!

Measure of Central Tendency Checkup – Key   Page 2

Name_____   Date_____

Find answers for each problem. (20 points each)

9. The Green Bay Packers scored the following points in their first seven games: 27, 42, 0, 13, 21, 27, and 10. Find the mean, median, mode, and range.

    Mean = 20   Median = 21   Mode = 27   Range = 42

10. Marissa got a new job. The first week she earned $130.25. The second week she earned $245.25. The third week she earned $238.75. This week she earned $312.75 Find the mean, median, mode, and range.

    Mean = $231.75   Median = $242.00   Mode = none   Range = $182.50

11. Andy wants his average bowling score to be no less than 120. The first game he bowled a 98. The second game he got 110. What is the lowest score he can get on the third game to have at least a 120 average?

    152

12. Maria scored an average of 22 points in the first seven games of the basketball season. These are the scores for the first six games: 15, 18, 30, 12, 22, and 18. How many points did she score during the seventh game?

    39 points

13. Rosie hopes to sell an average of at least $980 of merchandise each day in her store this week. On Sunday she took in $820, on Monday $675, on Tuesday $1,200, on Wednesday $1,000, on Thursday $726 and on Friday $1,300. What is the least amount of money she needs to take in on Saturday to reach her goal?

    $1,139

14. You received these five grade in mathematics: 88, 100, 88, 92, and 64. What is the mean, median, and mode of your grades?

    Mean = 86.4   Median = 88   Mode = 88

Figure 6.12

7

Teacher-Made Tests and Rubrics

USING TEACHER-MADE TESTS

Teacher-made tests are important evaluation tools for student learning. Simply defined, a teacher-made test is an evaluation tool designed by a teacher for his or her students that can be used at any point during a unit of study. Often the most instructionally relevant tests are those created by a teacher for a specific group of students to emphasize important information about the concepts taught (Childs, 1989).

This type of assessment helps to focus a teacher's instruction because those concepts deemed most important to evaluate are also the concepts deemed most important to be learned. According to the National Council of Teachers of Mathematics (2000), assessment should result in informed teaching. The purpose of assessment is not only to monitor and evaluate but also to enhance the learning process.

When used for formative purposes—to help guide student learning and increase student achievement—teacher-made tests can positively affect student knowledge. Using test results to evaluate what students know and need to learn is valuable because the information gleaned from test results should guide classroom practices and instruction. The use of classroom data to modify instruction, coupled with the sharing of that data with students, can greatly affect student achievement (Jenkins, 1997).

According to Black and Wiliam (1998), when teacher-made tests are used as a formative tool, the levels of overall achievement rise. The biggest effect is usually seen with low-achieving students because these students typically benefit the most from guidance in discerning what they should focus on to increase learning and performance. Teaching and learning must be adjusted based on formative assessment results if evaluation is to influence achievement (Black & Wiliam, 1998).

Many tests overemphasize memorization and skills and underemphasize knowledge and the useful performance of skills. Assessment results should display an accurate picture of what students know and how they are able to use that knowledge. Authentic simulations and problems—such as asking students to determine the length of a fence needed to surround a yard—can increase students' intellectual involvement in a test. When this occurs, the result is a more accurate picture of the students' ability to use their knowledge to create solutions to realistic situations (Wiggins, 1992).

Krueger and Sutton (2002) published their belief that a variety of assessment tools are essential in the demonstration of student understanding. They indicated a shift in mathematics from measuring student knowledge of skills and procedures toward tasks that are an application of knowledge and skills to new situations. Authentic tasks should be an integral part of the assessment process and kept in mind when designing classroom assessments.

Wilson (2005) reminds us that classroom assessments should be designed and administered only for skills, concepts, and procedures that have already been taught. Although this may seem obvious, it is important to consider both when designing a new assessment tool and when reusing a tool that was designed in the past. During the assessment design process, teachers need to keep in mind that the goal is to have students show what they know.

CREATING A TEACHER-MADE TEST

There are several factors teachers should keep in mind when creating a test that assesses students' knowledge and skills and that is beneficial for improving instruction. Burke (2005) cautions educators that teacher-made tests all too often emphasize lower level thinking. The creation of a good test can be time consuming and difficult. Quality control factors must be in place. Adhering to the suggestions that follow will assist in efforts to create a high-quality teacher-made test.

Standards

The purpose of any unit of study and evaluation should be rooted in standards. Standards provide focus by defining what it is that students are expected to know, what they should be able to do, and how they are to apply that knowledge. Standards provide direction not only for teaching and learning but also for assessment. A clear focus should be apparent at the onset of unit planning. Teachers need to consider the following questions:

- What knowledge should students have by the end of the unit of study?
- What knowledge is essential to the learning process?
- How should students be able to apply the knowledge?

Teacher-made tests should be developed around the answers to these three questions.

Tests should be created before the unit of study begins. This practice provides focus for developing classroom activities and guides what should be taught and what should be learned. Various strategies can be planned to meet the needs of all learners. For example, a teacher may decide that cooperative grouping may assist in the learning process or that graphic organizers would be useful in helping students organize thoughts, practices, and principles. Standards and goals should be shared with students prior to beginning the material so that students clearly understand expectations. The planning grid in Figure 7.1 can be used in the process of test development and to provide focus for the key content. Teachers can fill this out before beginning a unit to help clarify the goals of the teaching and learning.

Questions on a Teacher-Made Test

After standards and concepts have been defined and learning expectations are clear, the next step is to choose the types of questions to be used on the test. Questions should be varied to allow students to demonstrate their knowledge through various forms of questioning. Using different types of questions also allows teachers to get a clearer picture of student understanding. Some students are able to perform better on a specific type of question, and varying question types give students a better opportunity to excel at the task. Common types of questions include multiple choice, matching, completion, true-false, short answer, and essay. All types of questions do not need to be on every test, but all tests should include questions that allow students to apply their skills to problems that demonstrate understanding. When writing test questions, clarity is crucial. Students need to understand what they are expected to demonstrate when they are completing their response.

Figure 7.2 offers some tips teachers can use to construct questions that elicit student understanding. As summarized in the figure, when developing true-false questions, teachers should avoid words such as *all, never,* and *always* because these absolute words tend to confuse students. Students may know the material but get the answer wrong because of that confusion. Matching questions should be limited to 5 to 10 items so that the physical part of matching does not confuse the test taker. When multiple-choice questions are used, the main idea should be stated in the core of the sentence; doing so focuses the test-taker on the core knowledge needed to answer the question. Multiple correct answers can be offered to challenge students to evaluate the choices at a greater depth and to prevent students from simply guessing at which answer might be correct. When teachers create completion questions, they should avoid citing passages directly from their students' textbooks. Using textbook passages emphasizes memorization rather than higher order thinking. Finally, with essay questions, it is important to define the criteria for evaluation so students clearly understand what they are being asked to explain. It is also beneficial to use higher order thinking verbs—such as *evaluate, prediction, compare and contrast,* and *create*—rather than verbs that rely specifically on recall memory—such as *define, list,* or *name.*

Essential Knowledge Planning Grid

Standards: _____

Concepts: _____

Students are expected to: _____

Know	Do	Understand

Figure 7.1

Evaluating a Teacher-Made Test

After formulating test questions, a teacher can compare them to the Essential Knowledge Planning Grid (Figure 7.1) to be sure the questions address the goals of teaching. Then, the teacher can consider the following questions to be sure that the test includes all the information necessary to be a successful evaluation:

• Do the questions provide students with ample opportunity to demonstrate their grasp of the knowledge essential to key concepts?

• Does the successful completion of the assessment provide true evidence of understanding?

• At what level will students need to perform for the outcome to be deemed a success?

• What plans will be implemented for students who are unable to demonstrate a successful level of performance?

• What strategies will be employed to assist students in gaining a deeper understanding of concepts crucial to their success?

After answering these questions, the teacher can use the Test Construction Rubric (see Figure 7.3) to further evaluate the test. The criteria listed on the rubric were gathered from several sources, including educational Web sites, educational books, and educators themselves, and have been deemed important to the test construction, implementation, and evaluation process. Teachers can rate their test by comparing it to each of the various criteria.

Sharing Test Results

Timely constructive feedback is important to the formative assessment process so that students are still close to the learning and so that teachers can address any confusion on the part of students while the learning is still fresh in the students' minds. Written comments that assist students with improving their performance are beneficial. Such comments should be positive and nonjudgmental and should state what the student has completed and what still needs to be done to fulfill the assessment goal. For example, the feedback, "You have clearly explained what the word *mean* refers to; now, can you provide an example showing how to calculate the mean?" is more supportive than "You didn't give an example." Class discussions or a feedback session can be held when common misunderstandings arise among students. Students can provide insight into their thinking and the teacher can eliminate misconceptions and strengthen understandings.

Encourage students to think about and evaluate their own thinking. Martinez (2006) believes that for students to truly understand, thinking must become automatic, almost without conscious effort. It is through this automaticity that learning is demonstrated. He states that metacognition is an example of automaticity.

Tips for Constructing Test Questions

True-False Questions

- Avoid absolute words like *all, never,* and *always.*
- Make sure items are clearly true or false rather than ambiguous.
- Limit true-false questions to ten.
- Consider asking students to make false questions true to encourage higher-order thinking.

Matching Questions

- Limit list to between five and ten items.
- Use homogeneous lists (e.g., do not mix names with dates).
- Give clear instructions.
- Give more choices than there are questions.

Multiple-Choice Questions

- State main idea in the core or stem of the question.
- Use reasonable incorrect choices (i.e., avoid ridiculous choices).
- Make options the same length (nothing very long or very short).
- Include multiple correct answers (e.g., "A and B," "All of the above").

Completion Questions

- Structure for a brief, specific answer for each item.
- Avoid passages lifted directly from text (doing so emphasizes memorization).
- Use blanks of equal length.
- Avoid multiple blanks that sometimes make a sentence too confusing.

Essay Questions

- Avoid all-encompassing questions (e.g., ambiguous items such as "Discuss . . ." and "Tell all you know . . .").
- Define criteria for evaluation.
- Give point value.
- Use some higher order thinking verbs—such as *evaluate, predict, compare and contrast,* and *create* rather than all recall verbs—such as *define, list,* and *name.*

Figure 7.2

Adapted from *How to Assess Authentic Learning,* by Kay Burke. © 1999 Corwin Press. Reprinted by permission of Corwin Press, Thousand Oaks, CA.

According to the U.S. Department of Education (1993), sharing test results with students is an important part of the test-taking process. Students need to understand their strengths and evaluate their weaknesses. Students also must understand errors and be given the opportunity to ask questions and clarify misconceptions.

Test Construction Rubric *Points to Consider*	Needs work	Some evidence	Definitely
The test is linked directly to the standards and benchmarks.			
The test was created before teaching the unit.			
The language is appropriate to the task and the age level of the students.			
There are clear written directions for each section of the test.			
The types of test questions are varied and illustrate what students know and can do, and the questions contain applications to demonstrate understanding.			
The level of questioning is varied, and questions are arranged from easy questions to those that are more complex.			
Point values are listed for each section of the test.			
Students are expected to show their calculations or methods for obtaining answers.			
Sufficient time is allotted for completion of the test.			
Plans for evaluating and using test results are outlined in advance.			

Needs work Indicates that the expectation has not been met or is a weak illustration of that aspect of the test.

Some evidence Indicates that the expectation has been met but needs expansion or extension to better meet criteria.

Definitely Indicates that every expectation has been met and the result is an exemplary example of the criteria.

Figure 7.3

RUBRIC/MATHEMATICS APPLICATION

FINDING LCM AND GCF

This application covers the concepts of prime factorization, least common multiple (LCM), and greatest common factor (GCF). These concepts are foundational pieces that provide connections to understanding several mathematical operations. During the application, students will illustrate methods used to find LCM and GCF.

A teacher-made test is included with the chapter. The test can be used for formative or summative purposes. Using it in conjunction with the mathematics application helps students better understand the related mathematics concepts and ways that they apply the concepts to real-world situations.

Performance Task Explanation

People often learn best by doing, and they are able to increase their understanding when they explain something to others. In this task, students are asked to explain two methods of finding LCM and GCF to others. Their explanation includes illustrations of both methods and an example of a real-world application of the concept. An overview is provided in Figure 7.4, and a task explanation and suggested procedures are provided in Figure 7.5. Students will need to be introduced to both methods and be given the opportunity to practice before the task begins. After completing the task, students should be prepared to discuss which method they prefer and justify their answer. This application takes one or two 45-minute class periods.

The task could look like the examples in Figure 7.6. Students should be given the opportunity to be creative, however.

Figure 7.5 **Figure 7.6a** **Figure 7.6b** **Figure 7.7**

Rubric

Before beginning the task, students should be given a copy of the task (Figure 7.4) and the rubric (Figure 7.7). The rubric will guide students through the task. Being aware of criteria and expectations helps raise the level of performance.

Expanding the Task

When tasks are complete, students should be capable of teaching the concepts to other students. They should be very comfortable with prime factorization and finding GCF and LCM. At this point, the students could be paired with students from another mathematics class at the same or a different grade level. Students could then illustrate and explain the processes to others, as well as discuss some real-life applications.

Simplifying the Task

To simplify, the task could be limited to one concept. Students could be expected to illustrate either prime factorization, finding the GCF, or finding the LCM.

Unit Overview

Finding LCM and GCF

Standards:	Numbers and Operations, Problem Solving, Communication, Connections
Mathematics concepts:	Prime factorization, Least Common Multiple, Greatest Common Factor
Grade levels:	3 through 9
Related curricular areas:	Language arts—Writing an explanation; Art—creating a visual display
Materials:	Construction paper, rulers
Task:	Ms. Ellers is a mathematics teacher who needs your help. Her students have been learning about the Least Common Multiples (LCM) and Greatest Common Factors (GCF), but they get confused. She would like student input to decide the best method to teach and the best way to illustrate procedures.

Suggested Student Procedures

1. Create a visual display illustrating
   a. Two methods that can be used to find the Greatest Common Factor (GCF) of two numbers. First use the factor tree method, and then use the multiples listing method.
   b. Two methods that can be used to find the Least Common Multiple for two numbers. First use the factor tree method, and then use the factor listing method.

2. Include a written explanation of each method. Include an example of a real-life application for both.

3. Explain which method you prefer and why.

Teacher Resources

Task Explanation and Suggested Procedure page

Project Example pages

Rubric

Prime Factorization/LCM/GCF Checkup pages and Keys

Internet Resources

The Math Forum Internet Mathematics Library: Features links to mathematics resources, teaching strategies, and mathematics topics for various education levels. (http://www.forum.swarthmore.edu/library)

AAA Math: Contains lessons on many topics for teachers. (http://www.aaamath.com)

MathStories.com: Features more than 4,000 mathematics word problems to help grade school students improve their problem-solving skills. (http://www.mathstories.com)

Figure 7.4

Figure 7.8a   **Figure 7.8b**   **Figure 7.9a**   **Figure 7.9b**

Checkup (Teacher-Made Test)

Students are expected to understand the concepts of prime factorization, GCF, and LCM. They manipulate numbers and solve problems that illustrate how well they are able to apply their skills.

The assessment in Figure 7.8 includes the important components of a teacher-made test. The types of questions are varied, each section indicates the point value that is available for each question, directions are given for each section of the test, and the level of questioning is varied.

Students are asked to show all work needed to complete their answers. This can be done on the assessment or on a separate sheet of paper that is then attached to the test.

Test results should be shared with students as soon as possible. Teachers should explain any concepts that the test has shown to be unclear or confusing to students. If necessary, reteaching should take place, and students should be given additional opportunities to demonstrate their abilities.

A key to the assessment is provided in Figure 7.9.

IN SUMMARY

Well-constructed teacher-made tests can guide the instruction process by highlighting the important concepts of a unit for teaching and learning purposes. Constructing a test based on standards before a unit of study begins helps maintain a clear focus throughout, and using test results to guide instruction increases the level of student achievement.

Finding LCM and GCF

Task Explanation and Suggested Procedures

Task:

Ms. Ellers is a mathematics teacher who needs your help. Her students have been learning about Least Common Multiples (LCM) and Greatest Common Factors (GCF), but they get confused. She would like student input to decide the best method to teach and the best way to illustrate procedures.

Suggested Procedures:

1. Create a visual display illustrating:

   a. Two methods that can be used to find the Greatest Common Factor (GCF) of two numbers. First use the factor tree method, and then use the multiples listing method.

   b. Two methods that can be used to find the Least Common Multiple (LCM) for two numbers. First use the factor tree method, and then use the factor listing method.

2. Include a written explanation of each method. Include an example of a real-life application for both.

3. Explain which method you prefer and why.

Figure 7.5

Finding LCM and GCF

Project Example   **Page 1**

LCM Tree Method

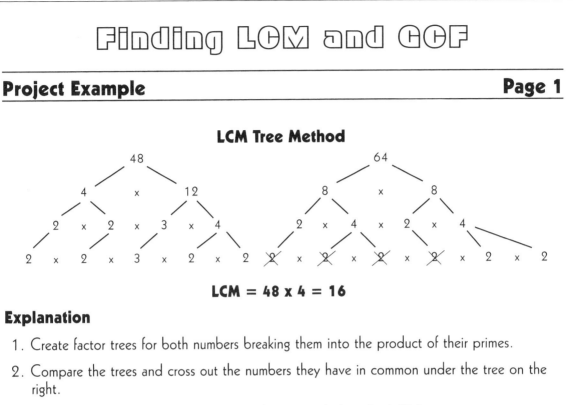

LCM = 48 x 4 = 16

Explanation

1. Create factor trees for both numbers breaking them into the product of their primes.

2. Compare the trees and cross out the numbers they have in common under the tree on the right.

3. Multiply all numbers that are not crossed out to calculate the LCM.

Real-world Application Example: (examples will vary)

LCM Multiples Method

Multiples of 48

    48   96   144 192 240 288 336 384 . . .

Multiples of 64

    64   128 192 . . .

LCM = 192

Explanation

1. List several multiples of the first number.

2. Continue to list multiples of the second number until you find the common multiple.

3. If one is not found, continue listing multiples of both numbers.

Real-world Application Example (examples will vary)

Figure 7.6   *(Continued)*

Finding LCM and GCF

Project Example   **Page 2**

GCF Tree Method

$$GCF = 2 \times 2 \times 2 \times 2 = 2^4 = 16$$

Explanation

1. Create factor trees for both numbers breaking them into the product of their primes.

2. Compare the trees and locate the common numbers.

3. Multiply one set of the common numbers to find the GCF.

Real-World Application Example: (examples will vary)

GCF Factor Method

48				**64**		
1	x	48		1	x	64
2	x	24		2	x	32
3	x	16		4	x	16
4	x	12		8	x	8
6	x	8				

1, 2, 3, 4, 6, 8, 12, (16,) 24, 48   1, 2, 4, 8, (16,) 32, 64

$$GCF = 16$$

Explanation

1. List all of the factors of both numbers.

2. Compare factors to find the largest number they have in common.

Real-World Application Example: (examples will vary)

Method I Prefer: (examples will vary)

Figure 7.6

Finding LCM and GCF

Rubric

Least Common Multiple and Greatest Common Factor

Highlight the descriptor that most accurately describes the product. Add points to gain final score.

	0	1	2	3
LCM Tree Method Trees	Incomplete or not present	Inaccurate	Correct	Correct, neat, easy to read
LCM	Not present	Inaccurate	Correct	Correct, labeled with LCM= _____
Explanation	Not present or inaccurate	Difficult to understand	Clear and accurate	Clear, accurate, perfect spelling and punctuation
LCM Multiples Method Factor Lists	Not present or inaccurate	Accurate with 2 or more multiples missing	Accurate with 1 multiple missing	Accurate and complete
LCM	Not present	Inaccurate	Correct	Correct, labeled with LCM= _____
Explanation	Not present or inaccurate	Difficult to understand	Clear and accurate	Clear, accurate, perfect spelling and punctuation
GCF Tree Method Trees	Incomplete or not present	Inaccurate	Correct	Correct, neat, easy to read
GCF	Not present	Inaccurate	Correct	Correct, labeled with GCF= _____
Explanation	Not present or inaccurate	Difficult to understand	Clear and accurate	Clear, accurate, perfect spelling and punctuation
GCF Factor Method Factor Lists	Not present or inaccurate	Accurate with 2 or more factors missing	Accurate with 1 factor missing	Accurate and complete
GCF	Not present	Inaccurate	Correct	Correct, labeled with GCF= _____
Explanation	Not present or inaccurate	Difficult to understand	Clear and accurate	Clear, accurate, perfect spelling and punctuation
Neatness	Sloppy	Difficult to read without careful concentration	Neat	Neat and attractive

Evaluator: _____   Points possible = 39   Points earned = _____

Figure 7.7

Finding LCM and GCF

Prime Factorization/LCM/GCF Checkup   Page 1

Name _____   Date _____

Choose the letter of the correct answer. Show all work. (3 points each)

1. What is the prime factorization of 16?
   a.) $2 \times 2 \times 2 \times 2$ b.) 4×4 c.) 2×8 d.) 8^2

2. What is the prime factorization of 64?
   a.) 8×8 b.) 2×32 c.) $2 \times 2 \times 2 \times 2 \times 2$ d.) 2^6

3. What is the LCM of 16 and 64?
   a.) 16   b.) 8   c.) 64   d.) 128

4. What is the GCF of 16 and 64?
   a.) 4   b.) 8   c.) 16   d.) 64

Write the letter of the correct answer on the line. Show all work. (3 points each)

_____	5. prime factorization of 120	a. $2^2 \times 5^2$
_____	6. prime factorization of 100	b. 75
_____	7. prime factorization of 144	c. 20
_____	8. LCM of 25 and 75	d. 30
_____	9. GCF of 60 and 80	e. 122
_____	10. LCM of 60 and 80	f. $2^3 \times 3 \times 5$
		g. $2 \times 3^2 \times 5$
		h. 10^2
		i. 240
		j. $2^4 \times 3^2$
		k. 150

Figure 7.8

(Continued)

Finding LCM and GCF

Prime Factorization / LCM / GCF Checkup   **Page 2**

Name _____   Date_____

Fill in the blanks with the word you feel would best complete the sentence. (10 points each)

11. 2^2 x 3 is the _____ (2 words) of the number 12.

12. 12 is the _____ (3 words) of 24 and 36.

13. 12 is the _____ (3 words) of 4 and 6.

Calculate and explain your answer. (20 points each)

14. Mr. Jackson has noticed that every fifth customer that enters his store buys bread. Every ninth person entering the store purchases milk. If Mr. Jackson has 120 customers enter his store today, how many will buy both milk and bread?

_____

_____

_____

_____

15. You are in charge of telling planes when to take off at Ames International Airport. The airport has decided that planes will take off on runway A every 15 minutes. Planes will take off on runway B every 10 minutes. Evaluate any problem this system might create. Discuss possible solutions.

_____

_____

_____

_____

Points possible = ___100___   Points earned = _____   Grade = _____

Figure 7.8

Finding LCM and GCF

Prime Factorization / LCM / GCF Checkup – Key   Page 1

Name _____   Date_____

Choose the letter of the correct answer. Show all work. (3 points each)

1. What is the prime factorization of 16?
   (a.) $2 \times 2 \times 2 \times 2$ b.) 4×4 c.) 2×8 d.) 8^2

2. What is the prime factorization of 64?
   a.) 8×8 b.) 2×32 c.) $2 \times 2 \times 2 \times 2 \times 2$ (d.) 2^6)

3. What is the LCM of 16 and 64?
   a.) 16   b.) 8   (c.) 64)   d.) 128

4. What is the GCF of 16 and 64?
   a.) 4   b.) 8   (c.) 16)   d.) 64

Write the letter of the correct answer of the line. Show all work. (3 points each)

f _____ 5. prime factorization of 120   a. $2^2 \times 5^2$

a _____ 6. prime factorization of 100   b. 75

j _____ 7. prime factorization of 144   c. 20

b _____ 8. LCM of 25 and 75   d. 30

c _____ 9. GCF of 60 and 80   e. 122

i _____ 10. LCM of 60 and 80   f. $2^3 \times 3 \times 5$

                                        g. $2 \times 3^2 \times 5$

                                        h. 10^2

                                        i. 240

                                        j. $2^4 \times 3^2$

                                        k. 150

Figure 7.9

(Continued)

Finding LCM and GCF

Prime Factorization / LCM / GCF Checkup – Key   Page 2

Name _____   Date_____

Fill in the blanks with the word you feel would best complete the sentence. (10 points each)

11. 2^2 x 3 is the ____prime factorization____ (2 words) of the number 12.

12. 12 is the ____greatest common factor____ (3 words) of 24 and 36.

13. 12 is the ____least common multiple____ (3 words) of 4 and 6.

Calculate and explain your answer. (20 points each).

14. Mr. Jackson has noticed that every fifth customer that enters his store buys bread. Every ninth person entering the store purchases milk. If Mr. Jackson has 120 customers enter his store today, how many will buy both milk and bread?

_____There will be two customers that buy both bread and milk. The two common multiples_____

_____of 5 and 9 up to 120, are 45 and 90._____

_____

_____

15. You are in charge of telling planes when to take off at Ames International Airport. The airport has decided that planes will take off on runway A every 15 minutes. Planes will take off on runway B every ten minutes. Evaluate any problem this system might create. Discuss possible solutions.

_____The planes will meet at the intersection of the runways every thirty minutes._____

_____Solutions will vary._____

_____

_____

Points possible = ____100____   Points earned= _____   Grade= _____

Figure 7.9

Using Rubric Data

ANALYZING DATA

Teachers need to become proficient and comfortable with the analysis of a variety of assessment data. When data are analyzed effectively, teachers can create a picture of student understanding. Rubric data add to the variety of assessment data teachers can view and interpret.

Data are increasingly available in schools. Petrides (2006) encouraged teachers to use it constructively. Rubrics are an incredible source of data, but they are often not used when evaluating individual and group performance.

When using an analytic rubric, the results create a clear picture of performance for students. By analyzing their score for each criterion or standard, students can identify their strengths and challenges. By reading the descriptors, students can visualize the steps necessary to accomplish higher levels of achievement.

The analysis of rubric results is always valuable. The value can be increased greatly, however, when the data are collected and viewed in a variety of ways. Data collection is most appropriate with projects, benchmark assessments, or common assessments.

INDIVIDUAL GRAPHS

Student data can be represented using a simple bar graph. A graph creates a powerful visual representation of student performance, highlighting high and low points of the performance as well as growth over time when appropriate.

For example, suppose students have just completed a benchmark assessment in which creating a graph was a key component and are evaluated by the rubric in Figure 8.1.

The graph in Figure 8.2 illustrates the scores Maria achieved on the graph she created for her benchmark assessment. It is easy to see Maria's areas of weakness and strength when viewing the graph. Although Maria had good results with the actual graphing, she had problems with the titles. Other errors were minor and, by viewing the rubric, Maria can better understand what she needs to do to improve her performance.

The graph can be created using Microsoft Excel. Data can be entered using the format illustrated in Figure 8.3.

Although the teacher may want to create the results graph, students can be asked to graph their results. Students can use graph paper, as in the original student graph, or they can create the graph electronically.

	1	2	3	4
Graph title	Partially or inaccurately titled **X**	Title not related to graph	Title related to graph	Title related to graph Perfect mechanics
Axes title	Incomplete or illegible titles	Titles present but unrelated to axes data **X**	Titles present and related to axes data	Titles present and related to axes data Perfect mechanics
x-axis information	Incomplete or illegible information	Labels or numbers present with partial inaccuracies	Labels or numbers present and accurate	Labels or numbers present and accurate and easy-to-read **X**
y-axis information	Incomplete or illegible information	Labels or numbers present with partial inaccuracies	Labels or numbers present and accurate	Labels or numbers present and accurate and easy-to-read **X**
Key	Incomplete	Complete with inaccuracies	Complete and accurate **X**	Complete, accurate, easy to read
Graphed according to key	No correspondence to key	Much graphed inaccurately	Graphed with minor error	Graphed according to key **X**
Accuracy of graph	Mostly inaccurate	Some inaccuracies	1 inaccuracy **X**	Completely accurate

Figure 8.1

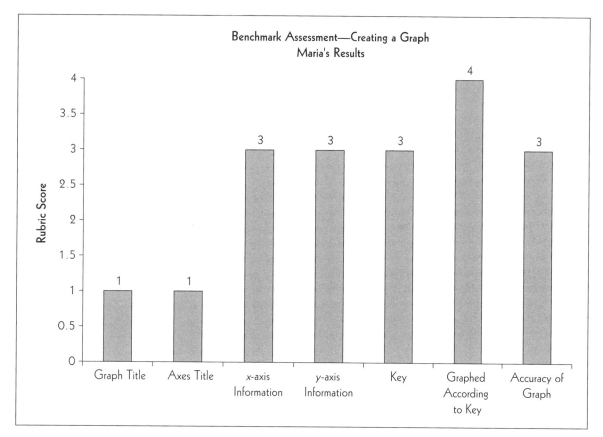

Figure 8.2

	Graph Title	Axes Title	x-axis Information	y-axis Information	Key	Graphed According to Key	Accuracy of Graph
Maria	1	1	3	3	3	4	3
Jorge	2	2	4	4	4	3	3
Melvin	1	1	4	3	3	3	3
Sally	1	1	2	1	1	1	1
Paul	3	2	2	2	3	2	2
John	2	2	3	3	3	3	3
Latitia	1	1	2	2	1	1	1
Juanita	2	2	3	3	3	3	3
Chelsea	1	2	3	3	4	4	4
Brittany	2	1	3	3	3	3	3
Cindy	2	2	3	4	4	4	4
Jeffrey	1	1	3	3	4	3	3

Figure 8.3

GROUP AND SUMMARY INFORMATION

To view class information, several students can be placed on the same graph. This helps the teacher view patterns in the assessment results. Figure 8.4 shows the results of the students. By comparing the bar lines, the teacher can see the strengths and deficits of each student. In Figure 8.5, the results are graphed by rubric category. This method better illustrates the areas of concern for the entire class, if such areas exist.

Figure 8.5 clearly illustrates that the class had more difficulty with the titles on their graphs compared to the other skill areas. This would be an indication to the teacher that additional time or practice needs to be spent clarifying misunderstandings in this area.

To take another look at class performance, class averages can be graphed. Figure 8.6 illustrates the average class performance on the assessment.

Again, it is evident that although students on average were nearly proficient in Categories 3 through 7, Categories 1 and 2 were a struggle for them, indicating additional instruction is necessary.

Figure 8.4

Figure 8.5

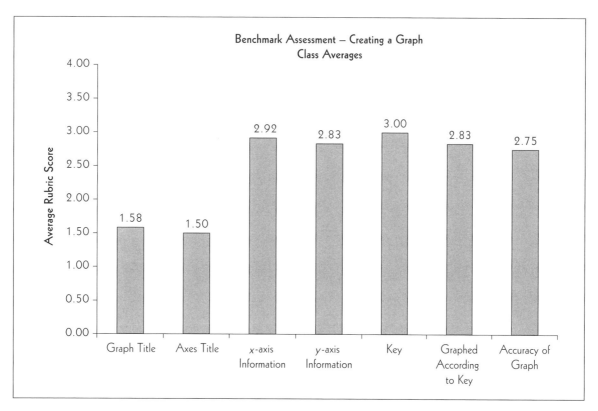

Figure 8.6

STUDENT COMPARISONS

Typically, when using rubrics, students are interested in their own results and what they need to do to achieve higher levels of performance. The occasion may arise, though, when it is beneficial for students to see results compared to the class average. In this case, a graph like the one in Figure 8.7 can be generated.

This graph creates a picture of individual student performance compared to the other students in class. Students will need only their results, the rubric, and possibly additional instruction to improve. Knowing the class average will not guarantee individual improvement, but it does create a comparative picture for the student.

Another comparison with a great deal of value is depicted in Figure 8.8. The information in this graph shows student performance over time. The graph serves to remind students of previous performance and can indicate growth or lack of increased performance. In addition, students are provided with a visual of strengths and challenges.

Figure 8.7

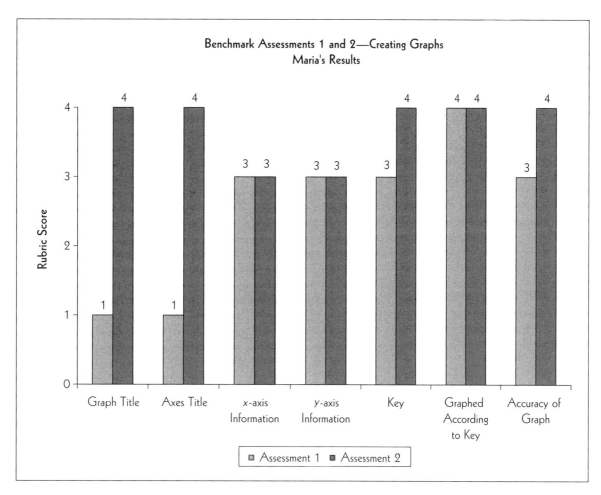

Figure 8.8

RUBRIC/MATHEMATICS APPLICATION

THE GARDEN

This application is most appropriate for students who are at or above Grade 3 and are familiar with area and perimeter.

Performance Task Explanation

In this application, students are asked to create a garden. To complete the application students are asked to find the area of parts of the garden while staying within certain overall dimensions. In addition, they need to find the perimeter of the garden. This task takes one to two 45-minute class periods. The time commitment depends on the grade level. Figure 8.9 provides an overview.

To begin the performance task, students need to determine the shape of a garden with an area of 48 square yards. After determining the overall dimensions, students divide the

Figure 8.9

garden into six or more smaller dimensions to plant vegetables of their choice. Students are asked to calculate the amount of fencing needed to surround the garden. They construct their gardens visually on Figure 8.10 while Figures 8.11 and 8.12 help them categorize their plan elements.

Figure 8.10   **Figure 8.11**   **Figure 8.12**

Students create a diagram of their garden, including the measurements of all divisions within the garden. The area of each section of the garden is calculated and placed on a chart to organize the information.

After completing all calculations, students explain the choices they made to complete the task. This explanation is in paragraph form.

Figure 8.13   **Figure 8.14**

Rubric

Students should always be aware of the characteristics of success when beginning an application. To meet and exceed the expectations for the task, students need to be aware of all aspects of the performance. Standards and expectations should be clear from the beginning to eliminate any confusion. Reviewing the task components as a class is helpful. Give students time to ask questions.

When completing the rubric (Figure 8.13), place an X at the point value achieved for each criterion listed on the rubric, or highlight the point value. Point values are added to determine the overall rubric score.

Figure 8.15   **Figure 8.16**   **Figure 8.17**

Expanding the Task

To expand the performance task, students can determine the number of plants that their garden can contain. This would require research into the amount of space needed for each plant thereby finding how many plants could be planted in each section of the garden. Research can also take place to determine the type and cost of fencing as well as the cost of the plants.

Students can also be encouraged to divide their garden into sections of a variety of shapes and sizes. A requirement might be that no two areas within the garden be the same dimensions.

Simplifying the Task

To simplify the performance task, students can be given possible dimensions to choose from to create a 48-square-foot garden. They can also be asked to create a garden of only rectangular shapes.

Viewing Rubric Results

As an additional task extension, students should be asked to complete a bar graph illustrating their personal rubric results.

IN SUMMARY

Collecting, organizing, and reporting rubric data increases the awareness of student levels of performance both individually and collectively. Viewing and evaluating assessment results leads to tailored instruction, which better meets the needs of the students. Data should be gathered and reported by students and used regularly by the students and the teacher to plan for future success. Data gathered and reported over time assist in evaluating progress and identifying problems throughout the years.

Unit Overview

The Garden

Standards:	Numbers and Operations, Geometry, Problem Solving, Communication, Connections
Mathematics concepts:	Area and perimeter
Grade levels:	3 to 8
Related curricular areas:	Language arts—writing an explanation
Materials:	Graph paper, rulers, computer access (optional)
Task:	Your family has asked you to design the layout for a large vegetable garden. They are letting you decide which vegetables are planted in the garden, but they are interested in variety and would like at least six different vegetables. The garden should be 48 square yards, but the actual dimensions are up to you. Because of a variety of animals in the area, you need to purchase fencing for the garden. You should determine how much fencing you need to completely surrounded the garden.

Suggested Student Procedures

1. Determine the dimensions of your garden. Decide which vegetables you will plant.

2. Create a diagram of the garden showing how the entire space will be used. Include the location of each type of vegetable to be planted.

3. Determine the area you will use for each vegetable.

4. Calculate the amount of fencing you need to surround the garden.

5. Write a brief essay about your garden. Tell why you chose your garden's dimensions and explain why you placed vegetables in certain locations and how you decided how much space to give each type of vegetable in the garden. Include an explanation of how you calculated the amount of fencing needed.

Teacher Resources

Task Explanation and Suggested Procedure page

Garden Design Grid and Sample

Organizational Tool for Garden Information and Sample

Garden Checklist

Rubric

Student Explanation page

Internet Resources

Cool Math: This site offers a variety of insights into geometry including polyhedra and tessellations. (www.coolmath4kids.com/tesspag1.html)

History of Geometry: This site includes a brief history of geometry dating back to ancient civilizations. (http://geometryalgorithms.com/history.htm)

A Plus Math: This page includes an interactive game that requires students to match geometric terms to pictures that illustrate the terms. (www.aplusmath.com)

Figure 8.9

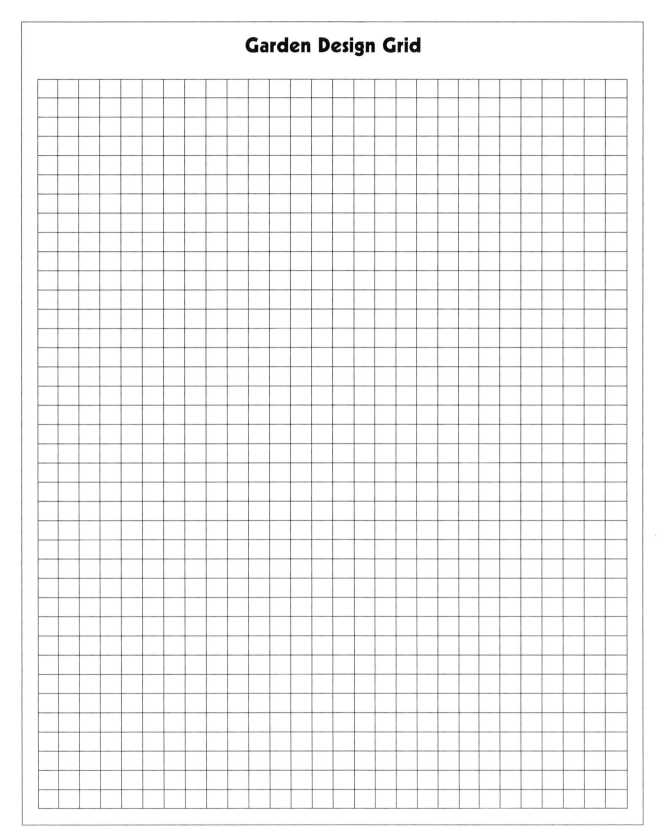

Garden Design Grid

Figure 8.10

Organizational Tool for Garden Information

Vegetable	Dimensions in the Garden (Yards)	Area for Vegetable (Square Yards)	Running Total of Areas (Square Yards)
Total of all areas combined			

Total of areas:

Length of fencing needed:

Width of fencing needed:

Total amount of fencing needed:

Figure 8.11

Garden Checklist

	Yes!	I'm working at it.
Is the area of my garden 48 square yards?		
Have I included at least six different vegetables?		
Is my garden diagram complete?		
Have I found the individual areas for each vegetable?		
Have I found the amount of fencing needed for my garden?		
Have I completed my explanatory paragraphs?		

Figure 8.12

Garden Task Rubric

	1	**2**	**3**	**4**
Garden area	Incomplete or incorrect	Complete Accurate	Complete Accurate Labeled	Complete Accurate Labeled Easy to read
Garden diagram	Incomplete or incorrect	Complete Accurate	Complete Accurate Labeled	Complete Accurate Labeled Easy to read
Vegetable areas	Mostly incomplete or incorrect	1 incomplete or inaccurate Labeled	Complete Accurate Labeled	Complete Accurate Labeled Easy to read
Perimeter for fencing	Incomplete or incorrect	Complete Accurate	Complete Accurate Labeled	Complete Accurate Labeled Easy to read
Explanation	Incomplete or incorrect	Complete Accurate Many mechanical errors	Complete Accurate Sentences clear and easy to understand 2 or 3 mechanical errors	Complete Accurate Sentences clear and easy to understand 1 mechanical error

Figure 8.13

Explanation: About My Garden

Figure 8.14

Garden Design Grid Sample

Figure 8.15

Organizational Tool for Garden Information Sample

Vegetable	Dimensions in the Garden (Yards)	Area for Vegetable (Square Yards)	Running Total of Areas (Square Yards)
Corn	3 yds × 6 yds	18 sq yds	18 sq yds
Tomatoes	3 yds × 3 yds	9 sq yds	27 sq yds
Onions	3 yds × 3 yds	9 sq yds	36 sq yds
Green peppers	2 yds × 2 yds	4 sq yds	40 sq yds
Green beans	2 yds × 2 yds	4 sq yds	44 sq yds
Banana peppers	2 yds × 2 yds	4 sq yds	48 sq yds
Total of all areas combined			

Total of areas:

    Length of fencing needed: 8 yards
    Width of fencing needed: 6 yards
    Total amount of fencing needed: 28 yards

Figure 8.16

Explanation: About My Garden

I chose the vegetables in my garden because my family likes those better than any others. I decided on the dimensions because it would really fit in my yard. I placed the vegetables the way I did because of the amount of each one that I wanted. For example, I knew that corn would take more space, and we really like corn, so I made that area the biggest.

I found the area by finding how many yards long each part of the garden is. Because the grid paper was in feet, I knew that 3 squares on the grid counted as 1 yard. After finding the yards, I multiplied the length and the width to find the number of square yards for that section. I did this for each section. Then I added the sections.

To find the fencing, I found how many yards the length and width were, then I multiplied the width by 2 and the length by 2 and added the numbers to get the fencing amount. The fencing is for the perimeter of the garden.

Figure 8.17

9

Mathematics and Communication

MATHEMATICAL VOCABULARY

Increased familiarity with mathematical vocabulary will help students in their efforts to express their thoughts. Creating common vocabulary is key when helping students understand mathematics. Teachers should promote the use of proper terms by modeling their use. Students are most likely to increase and understand vocabulary when it is used regularly and in context by the teacher. According to Marzano and Pickering (2005), when content area terminology is familiar to students, they are more likely to learn and understand the subject.

COMMUNICATION

According to Cawelti (2004), practices to improve students' learning include providing students with varied opportunities to communicate mathematically: Communication enhances understanding.

Rich and varied problems are valuable when helping students understand and apply mathematical concepts. Successfully completing these types of problems enhances mathematical understanding. In addition, to cement student understanding, students should be asked to communicate their solution process (see Figure 9.1). Students with a solid foundation, when asked to explain the process that led to their solution, are able to verbalize the path they took, why they chose that path, and how they arrived

How did I solve the problem?	
How do I know that my solution is accurate?	

Figure 9.1

at an answer. The explanation is an evaluation of student understanding. Only if students have a solid comfort level with concepts and procedures are they able to clearly verbalize the steps taken to successfully solve a task. Students should also be expected to communicate why they chose a particular path to their solution.

Teacher examples increase the likelihood of effective communication. When asked how they got an answer, students might simply say, "I did it in my head" or "I'm not sure; it just came to me." These responses do not increase the probability of a successful solution the next time a similar problem arises. Teachers should model acceptable responses: A clear, step-by-step explanation of the solution process should be modeled for various problems throughout the year. Students should have knowledge of the components of a valuable explanation. When outlining the solution process, students should be encouraged to verbalize methods they may have tried that didn't work. In doing so, students understand that persistence is sometimes necessary to arrive at correct solutions.

In addition to the solution process, students should be asked to evaluate and justify their answer. How do they know their solution is correct? Could another solution be correct as well or is there only one answer? How do they know that to be the case?

Teachers should begin encouraging student explanations in the early elementary grades. The depth of the explanation will increase as students proceed through the grades. Their method of communication will also change, and the variety of communication tools available to them will grow. Young students may verbalize or draw pictures to clarify their thoughts; older students may use these methods as well as writing.

A variety of tools should be available to students as they construct explanations. Simple supplies, such as calculators, rulers, grid paper, plain paper, colored pencils, and scissors, should be easily accessible. Computers and tape recorders, when available, are also helpful. Teachers should allow students to choose the tools they feel best help them complete their assignment.

Communication should be frequent, consistent, and a regular part of the classroom routine. Various opportunities to communicate should be provided each day, in verbal and written form. Students can be asked to explain, in verbal form, their solution to a partner or to the entire class.

In addition to verbal explanations, students can explain their thoughts through written words or drawings. Teachers can also increase the amount of written communication through the use of math logs or journals. Journaling, according to Bizar and Daniels (2005), can take students beyond the curriculum and help them think. Students can use their journals to react to a problem, explain a solution, or create problems that address standards.

Students can also practice math terminology by creating written math problems. After the class solves the student-created problems, the students can explain their solution verbally or in writing.

FEEDBACK

Feedback refers to information supplied to students about their performance. The purpose of feedback is to analyze student performance as it relates to the objectives of the assignment so that students can then analyze their own performance. Feedback provides students the information they need to create their own improvement path.

Protheroe et al. (2004), when discussing techniques to promote a positive attitude toward math, indicated that students should be told what they are doing well and where additional work is required. This type of feedback is not only helpful with students' academic progress but with their feelings toward math as well.

Timely feedback affects student success. For feedback to be a catalyst for improvement, students need feedback as soon after the completion of the assignment as possible. If tomorrow's success depends on today's performance, feedback should be given prior to the next assignment. Using teacher input, students can immediately make adjustments to better demonstrate their understanding in their next performance. When long-term projects are completed, feedback may take slightly longer to occur. A reasonable length of time should be considered, based on the task being evaluated, keeping in mind that timeliness is key.

Honesty is a crucial component when analyzing student work. False praise does not lead to enhanced student achievement. Rather, pointing out strengths and challenges tactfully and honestly, while guiding students toward achievement of standards and objectives, has great benefit.

Consistency and frequency are also important components of feedback. Responding to students' work on a regular basis promotes the probability of increased student performance. Consistent focus and expectations also add to positive student results.

Descriptive feedback provides students with a model to use for self-assessment. Self-assessment is an effective precursor to reflection and goal setting (Guskey, 2005).

REFLECTION

Student reflection is most likely to occur when the teacher provides time and direction. If reflection is an expectation, students should be given a format for reflection and the opportunity to reflect: What did I learn in class today? What questions do I have? What do I feel confident about? What is challenging for me? What help do I need to improve? When reflection is formalized, collected, and analyzed by the teacher, it can be used to tailor instruction to best meet the needs of the students.

Bizar and Daniels (2005) stated that teachers don't need to teach students what to think but rather how to think. Reflection can help teachers to obtain that result. Simple tools can be used to organize student reflections, such as those shown in Figures 9.2 and 9.3.

What did I do well?	How can I improve?

Figure 9.2

What did I learn?	
What confuses me?	
What help do I need?	

Figure 9.3

Regular teacher reflection leads to beneficial use of instructional strategies to best meet students' needs. The adjustment of content is also the logical result of reflection: Did students understand the content of today's lesson? How do I know? If they don't understand, what am I going to do about it? What will I do for students who already have a solid understanding of the concepts I am teaching?

Several simple activities can be used to promote reflection. The reflective exercises listed in this section will help students evaluate their mathematical progress.

Share-List Strategy

Place students in groups of four and have them take turns sharing key points from the lesson with their group. Allow 90 seconds to pass. Then give students an additional 90 seconds to list the key points they heard in their group sharing.

Think-Speak-Write Strategy

Have students spend 1 minute silently thinking of the key points they learned during the lesson. Then have them spend 1 minute sharing ideas with a partner (30 seconds each student). For the final minute, have students work independently to write a one-sentence summary of the key points discussed.

Give-Me-10 Strategy

Have students quickly find a partner and spend 1 minute sharing the key concepts learned in class. Then ask 10 volunteers to share one idea with the class. Ideas should not be repeated.

Two-Four-Eight Strategy

Have students share one key idea learned in class with a partner. Then have the pair join another pair to form a group of four students. Instruct each student in the group to share a key idea with the other members of the group. Direct two foursomes to join another to form a group of eight students. Each student then shares a key concept with the others.

Stand Up–Sit Down Strategy

Instruct all students in class to stand up. Ask volunteers to take turns sharing a key point from class. After the point is shared, tell the student to sit down. Then quickly call on another volunteer to share. The object of this reflection is to have as many students as possible sit down in a 3-minute period.

The Big Three Strategy

Provide students with an index card on which they respond to three statements: name one thing you learned today, list one thing that you liked about class today, and write one question that you have. When complete, collect the cards. Use the reflections to guide your planning for the next class.

Headline News Strategy

On an index card, ask students to write a headline that summarizes the main point of class. Underneath the headline, tell students to write a one-sentence summary of what they learned from the day's lesson. Students can also work with a partner in this activity.

Echo Strategy

Say a key word that had significance in the lesson. Tell students to repeat the word and then write a sentence explaining what it means or why it is significant. If the activity is done verbally, ask volunteers to repeat the word and state a sentence. Continue choosing new words as time allows.

Have a Ball Strategy

Instruct students to form a large circle around the room and spend 1 minute in silent reflection, taking time to recall the key messages from class. Then, toss a ball to a student who states one main point. Tell the student to toss the ball to another student, who states another key point. Continue this process as quickly as possible until time runs out.

2L-1Q Strategy

This strategy involves a written reflection. Provide students with a note card on which they write two things they learned during class and one question that they have about the lesson's content.

What Do I Think? Strategy

Ask students to create a two-column chart on a piece of paper. Tell students to write the task that they did well in the first column. Have them list anything they would do differently in the second column.

MATHEMATICS APPLICATION

SALES TAX TASK

The application that follows can serve several purposes. It helps students better understand a real-world use of percents and it gives them the opportunity to apply their skills in calculating percents. The task also provides an expanded view of the world and helps students realize that tax is not a constant but in fact varies from place to place. Internet skills are used to collect the data needed to fulfill the task requirements. The application overview is presented in Figure 9.4, and an organizational tool is shown in Figure 9.5.

Performance Task Explanation

Students are asked to choose eight cities in addition to their own city and use the city's tax rates to complete the task. Students need to research the amount of sales tax charged in each of the chosen cities, calculate the amount of money charged on a given purchase, and determine the total amount spent in each location.

To solidify their understanding, students are also asked to complete the following tasks:

1. Explain the procedure used to calculate the amount charged in sales tax
2. Detail the method used to determine the total spent
3. Compare the amount charged in each city
4. Reflect on the completed task

Rubric

After students are given the rubric, they will need time to view all criteria and descriptors to better understand the task (see Figure 9.6). Because viewing and understanding the rubric is directly tied to the successful completion of the task, class time should be provided to analyze the rubric. Rubrics, when used regularly, are better understood by the learner, though the criteria often vary from rubric to rubric. So, although it may take time to view rubric components, it is still a crucial task.

Expanding the Task

To make the task more challenging, instead of computing sales tax have students select various cities around the world and calculate the exchange rate in the currency for that country. Then have students determine the amount of money needed in each country to pay for the clothing.

Students can create their own chart including the name of the country and its currency, the current exchange rate, and the amount of American dollars needed to pay for the clothes.

Student procedural explanations will be similar, though students can include their thoughts about the best place to visit. Although some students may take a primarily financial approach and choose the location that costs the least, other students will come up with other valid reasons. Accept all reasoning, as long as it is clearly explained and logical.

Unit Overview

Sales Tax Task

Standards: Numbers and Operations, Problem Solving, Communication

Mathematics concepts: Whole number operations

Grade levels: 5 to 8

Related curricular areas: Technology—Internet research

Materials: Paper and pencil, computer with Internet access

Task: Ms. Ornowski went on a trip to Milwaukee, Wisconsin. Unfortunately, her luggage was lost. Because the airline told her it would take a few days to locate and return her luggage, Ms. Ornowski needed to buy some clothes. She went to a local mall and purchased $290 worth of clothing. Because of the local 5.5% sales tax, she actually paid more for her clothes. This got her wondering what she would have paid in other cities in the United States. To help satisfy her curiosity, choose eight U.S. cities plus your own. Find the amount of sales tax in each of the cities chosen and determine the total amount spent in each city.

Suggested Student Procedures

1. Choose eight cities in addition to your own. Find the amount of sales tax charged in each location.

2. Create a chart to illustrate the information you found. Include the name of the city, how or where the amount of tax was found, the percent of sales tax administered in the city, the amount of money the tax added to the bill, and the total amount paid for the clothes.

3. Complete the chart.

4. Explain how you found the amount of money paid for sales tax in each city. Tell how you determined the total amount of the sale.

5. Write a paragraph comparing the total amounts of money spent. Include your choice of the best location to purchase clothing. Explain why that location, in your opinion, is the best place to shop. Include thoughts on why the sales tax might be different in each location.

6. Complete the three-question refection.

Teacher Resources

Organizational Tool for Project Components page

Task Explanation and Suggested Procedure page

Steps in Determining Total Sale Example

Sales Tax Task Rubric

Internet Resources

Math League: This site offers a variety of tools and explanations for many math concepts. (http://www.mathleague.com/help/percent/percent.htm)

Math Goodies: This site includes several different math resources and a game using fractions, decimals, and percents. (http://www.mathgoodies.com/lessons/vol4/challenge_vol4.html)

Figure 9.4

Sales Tax Task

Organizational Tool for Project Components

Name of City	Tax Information Found	Percent of Sales Tax	Amount of Tax ($)	Total Amount Paid

Figure 9.5

Sales Tax Task

Rubric

	1	2	3	4	
City tax	1–5 cities and tax present	6 or 7 cities and tax present	8 or 9 cities and tax present	10 cities and tax present	× 1 = ___
Tax in dollars	1–5 correct	6 or 7 correct	8 or 9 correct	All correct	× 2 = ___
Total sale	1–5 correct	6 or 7 correct	8 or 9 correct	All correct	× 3 = ___
Explanation of procedure	Present but inaccurate	Accurate	Accurate Clearly stated	Accurate Clearly stated Example included	× 1 = ___
Paragraph and reflection	Present	Present All components included Clearly stated	Present All components included Clearly stated Sensible	Present All components included Clearly stated Sensible	× 1 = ___

Total points earned = _____

Figure 9.6

Simplifying the Task

Teachers can simplify the task by providing Internet sites for the students to visit. Doing so also saves time. Students can also use a chart or diagram to explain and illustrate the steps used in determining the total sales price (see Figure 9.7).

Communication

Students are asked to put their thoughts into writing to clarify ideas and solidify understanding. When students explain procedures, they demonstrate what they know and their level of knowledge.

Encourage students to share their explanations with each other. Provide students with multiple opportunities to discuss their thinking and the steps they have taken to complete the task. Through such discussions students will deepen their own understanding.

Sales Tax Task

Steps in Determining Total Sale—Example

Percent of Tax	Tax as Percent	Amount of Sale Before Tax	Sales Tax Calculation	Amount of Tax	Total Sale Calculation	Total Sale
5.5%	.055	$290.00	290 × 0.055 = 15.95	$15.95	290 + 15.95 = 305.95	$305.95

Figure 9.7

IN SUMMARY

Students need increased and varied opportunities to communicate mathematically. Clear, thoughtful explanations demonstrate student understanding. Providing students with chances to share their thoughts and ideas with others creates an atmosphere in which students can learn from each other.

Increased writing can be promoted in a variety of ways, including the use of logs or journals. Students can be asked to regularly explain procedures and solutions. Student-created math problems and test items provide opportunities for students to expand communication. Reflections and class discussions should be an ordinary part of the class routine.

Communication can be increased without difficulty through forethought and advance planning. Although it requires commitment and planning, frequent use of communication techniques can have incredible effects.

Appendix 1

*Additional Rubric/Mathematics
Application Projects*

The following are additional application projects that teachers can use in their classroom. Each project relates to National Council of Teachers of Mathematics (NCTM) standards and contains a project overview that describes the project and the resources needed to conduct the project. The worksheets and rubrics needed to carry out the project in the classroom are also included.

Project 1 Overview

Measurement and Statistics

Standards:	Measurement, Statistics (graphing), Communication, Problem Solving
Mathematics concepts:	Metric measurement of length, weight and diameter, and graphing
Grade levels:	2 through 7
Materials:	Metric rulers and scale, string, graph paper, mini pumpkins
Task:	Determine who has the largest pumpkin.

Suggested Student Procedures

1. Each individual or cooperative group will receive a pumpkin.

2. Discuss ways the largest pumpkin could be identified (weight, height, diameter). Choose a method for your group.

3. Using the proper measurement tool, find the measurement for each pumpkin in the group. (Diameter can be measured using a string and a ruler.)

4. Measurements can be made to the nearest centimeter and gram. Record all measurements on the chart.

5. Graph the data collected.

6. Complete the Reflections page.

Teacher Resources

Task Explanation and Suggested Procedures page (Figure A1.2)

Reflections page (Figure A1.3)

Rubric (Figure A1.4)

Example Graph (Figure A1.5)

Graph (blank, Figure A1.6)

Figure A1.1

Measurement and Statistics

Task Explanation and Suggested Procedures

Task: Determine who has the largest pumpkin.

Suggested Procedures:

1. Discuss the methods you could use to determine who has the biggest pumpkin.
2. Choose at least one method.
3. Collect and record group data.
4. Make a bar graph of the data. Make sure you include all of the needed information.
5. Complete the Reflections page independently.

Names of Group Members	Data Being Collected

Figure A1.2

Measurement and Statistics

Reflections

Describe the method your group chose to determine who had the largest pumpkin. Explain why that method was chosen.

_____

_____

_____

_____

_____

_____

_____

_____

What did you learn today?

_____

_____

_____

Was there something that you liked about math class today?

_____

_____

_____

Was there something that you would have done differently?

_____

_____

_____

Figure A1.3

Measurement and Statistics

Rubric

	0	1	2	3
Graph Title	No title	Title does not relate to the graph.	Title relates to graph. Capitalization or spelling error present.	Title relates to graph. Capitalization and spelling are perfect.
Axes Labeled	No labels	Labels do not relate to graph.	Labels relate to graph. Capitalization or spelling error present.	Labels relate to graph. Capitalization and spelling are perfect.
x-axis information	Not present	Information present but inappropriate.	Information present with errors.	Information present and accurate.
y-axis information	Not present	Axis numbered incorrectly.	Axis numbered correctly.	Axis numbered correctly and neatly.
Graph accuracy	Incomplete	Graph complete but inaccurate.	Graph complete and accurate.	Graph complete, accurate and neat.

Evaluator:_____   Points possible = 15   Points earned = _____

Figure A1.4

Measurement and Statistics

Example Graph

Not sure what goes where? Use this as a model.

The Great Pumpkin

Figure A1.5

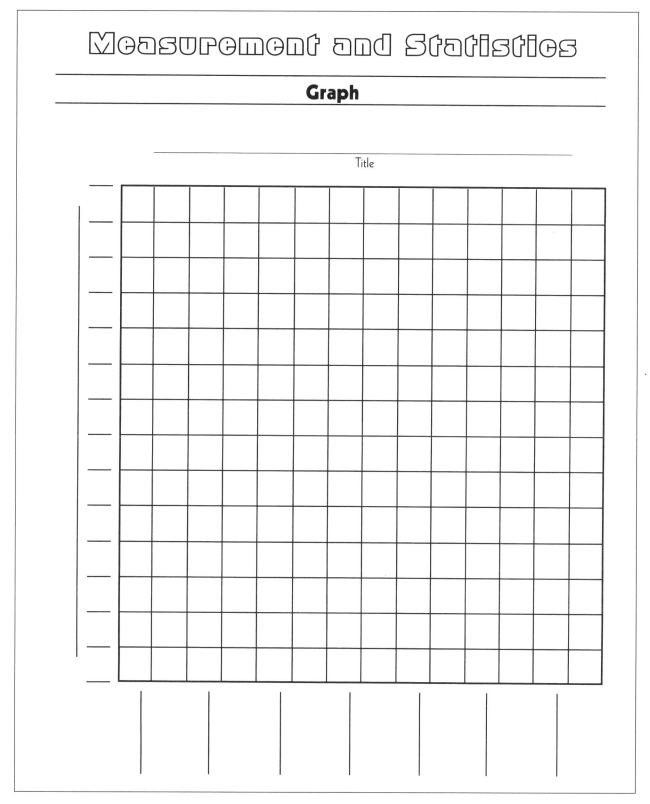

Measurement and Statistics

Graph

Title

Figure A1.6

Project 2 Overview

Symmetry and Area

Standards:	Geometry, Communication, Problem Solving
Mathematics concepts:	Symmetry and area
Grade levels:	4 through 10
Materials:	Graph paper, standard rulers
Task:	The Atlas Tile Company is looking for new 8-inch by 8-inch floor tile patterns. Company requirements say that all tiles must have at least one line of symmetry and be made of a variety of polygons with various sizes and shapes. Polygons should be covered with patterns to add interest to the floor tile. When the tile is complete, the people at Atlas need to know the exact area of each pattern in the tile. This will help with ordering meterials. They also need an explanation as to how much material will be needed to cover a 12-foot by 18-foot floor.

Suggested Student Procedures

1. Using an 8-inch by 8-inch piece of graph paper and a ruler, draw a mosaic tile. The tile should be made up of various polygons of different sizes and shapes and have at least one line of symmetry.

2. Shapes within the tile should be decorated with at least six different colors or patterns.

3. Determine the amount of each pattern or color needed to recreate the tile. (Find the area in square inches.)

4. Draw the tile and an organizational chart showing the patterns, formulas, and amount of material needed to complete each pattern within the tile.

5. Write an explanation telling the amount of each pattern needed to complete a 12-foot by 18-foot floor.

Teacher Resources

Sample Tile and Organizational Chart (Figure A1.8)

Sample Solution (Figure A1.9)

Rubrics (Figures A1.10 and A1.11)

Figure A1.7

Symmetry and Area

Sample Tile and Organizational Chart

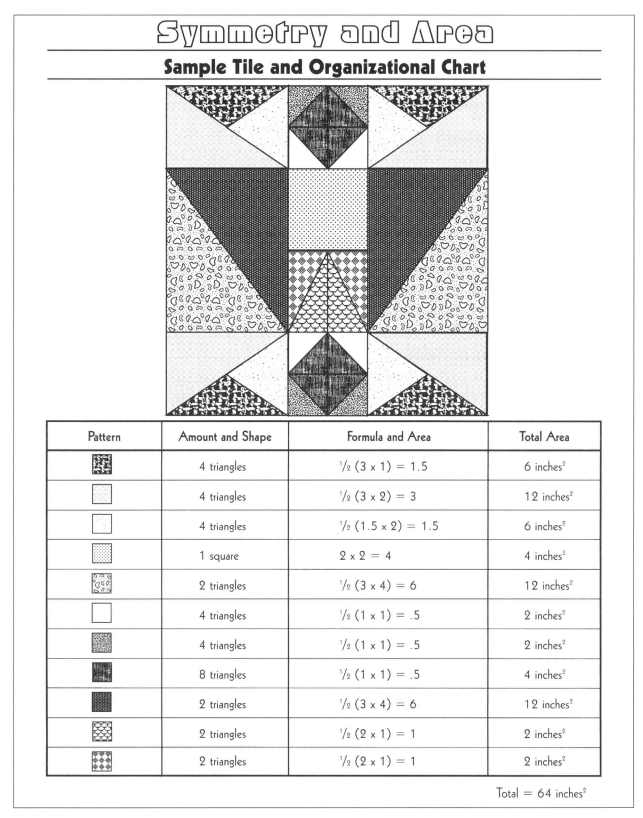

Pattern	Amount and Shape	Formula and Area	Total Area
	4 triangles	$\frac{1}{2}(3 \times 1) = 1.5$	6 inches^2
	4 triangles	$\frac{1}{2}(3 \times 2) = 3$	12 inches^2
	4 triangles	$\frac{1}{2}(1.5 \times 2) = 1.5$	6 inches^2
	1 square	$2 \times 2 = 4$	4 inches^2
	2 triangles	$\frac{1}{2}(3 \times 4) = 6$	12 inches^2
	4 triangles	$\frac{1}{2}(1 \times 1) = .5$	2 inches^2
	4 triangles	$\frac{1}{2}(1 \times 1) = .5$	2 inches^2
	8 triangles	$\frac{1}{2}(1 \times 1) = .5$	4 inches^2
	2 triangles	$\frac{1}{2}(3 \times 4) = 6$	12 inches^2
	2 triangles	$\frac{1}{2}(2 \times 1) = 1$	2 inches^2
	2 triangles	$\frac{1}{2}(2 \times 1) = 1$	2 inches^2

Total = 64 inches^2

Figure A1.8

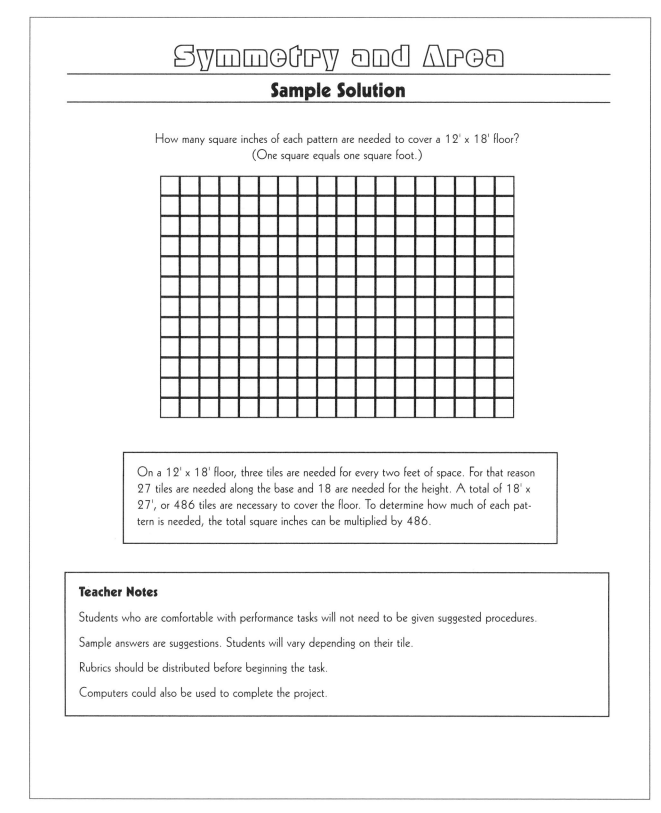

Symmetry and Area

Sample Solution

How many square inches of each pattern are needed to cover a 12' x 18' floor?
(One square equals one square foot.)

On a 12' x 18' floor, three tiles are needed for every two feet of space. For that reason 27 tiles are needed along the base and 18 are needed for the height. A total of 18' x 27', or 486 tiles are necessary to cover the floor. To determine how much of each pattern is needed, the total square inches can be multiplied by 486.

Teacher Notes

Students who are comfortable with performance tasks will not need to be given suggested procedures.

Sample answers are suggestions. Students will vary depending on their tile.

Rubrics should be distributed before beginning the task.

Computers could also be used to complete the project.

Figure A1.9

Symmetry and Area

Symmetry and Area Rubric

Highlight the descriptor for each criteria that best fits the product. Add points earned to determine total rubric score.

	1	2	3	4
Tile **Shapes and sizes**	4 or less different shapes or sizes used	5–6 different shapes or sizes used	7–8 different shapes or sizes used	9 or more different shapes or sizes used
Patterns	4 or less different patterns used	5–6 different patterns used	7–8 different patterns used	9 or more different patterns used
Line of Symmetry	Tile is not symmetrical	Not applicable	Not applicable	Tile has 1 or more lines of symmetry
Neatness	Sloppy; ruler or computer not used	Ruler or computer used, shapes overlap or have space in between	Ruler or computer used, shapes neatly aligned	Ruler or computer used, shapes neatly aligned, tile looks professional
Organizational Chart	Disorganized; doesn't contain formulas/equations, area, or patterns	Organized; some information missing (formulas/equations, area, or patterns)	Organized; patterns, formulas/ equations, and area information is present	Organized and neat; formulas/ equations, patterns, and area information are present
Formulas/Equations	3 or more missing or incorrect	All present, 1–2 incorrect	All present and correct and written accurately	All present, correct, written accurately and neatly
Areas	3 or more missing or incorrect	All present, 1–2 incorrect	All present and correct	All present and correct including inches²
Total Areas	3 or more missing or incorrect	All present, 1–2 incorrect	All present and correct	All present and correct including inches²

Student name: _____   Evaluator: _____   Points possible = 32   Points earned = _____

FIGURE A1.10

Symmetry and Area

Symmetry and Area Explanation Rubric

Highlight the descriptor for each criteria that best fits the product. Add points earned to determine total rubric score.

	1	2	3	4
Explanation Spelling and Grammar	4 or more spelling or grammar errors	2–3 spelling or grammar errors	1 spelling or grammar error	Spelling and grammar perfect!
Clarity	Difficult to understand	Unclear in parts	Clearly written	Clearly written, well explained
Neatness	Sloppy	Can be read with careful concentration	Neatly written	Neatly typed

Student Name: _____ Evaluator: _____ Points Possible = 12 Points earned = _____

Figure A1.11

Project 3 Overview

Standard Measurement

Standards:	Measurement, Communication, Problem Solving
Mathematics concepts:	Standard measurement of length and weight, area
Grade levels:	4 through 8
Materials:	Standard rulers and scale, graph paper, assorted stuffed beanbag animals
Task:	The Teenie Stuffed Critter Company needs to make more Teenie Stuffed Critters for giveaways for the Better Burger Corporation. To order materials, they need to know how much fabric and filler is needed to make the various critters.

Suggested Student Procedures

1. Each individual or cooperative group will receive beanbag animals.

2. Weigh each beanbag animal to the smallest unit possible with the scale provided.

3. Using $\frac{1}{4}$-inch graph paper and a ruler, draw a two-dimensional diagram of the beanbag animal and its parts. The diagram should include all pieces of fabric necessary to construct the toy and may be drawn in parts. The colors needed should be labeled for each part drawn.

4. Include all measurements to the nearest $\frac{1}{4}$ inch. Make as many measurements as necessary to accurately label all parts of the creature.

5. Use the measurements and the drawing to find the approximate amount of fabric needed for each part of the beanbag animal.

6. Create a chart including beanbag animal name, weight, colors, and amount of fabric needed. Attach it to the drawing.

7. Write a summary of your findings.

Teacher Resources

Sample Page (Figure A1.13)

Rubric (Figure A1.14)

Figure A1.12

Standard Measurement

Sample Page

Teenie Stuffed Critter: Nuts the Squirrel   Weight = _____ ounces

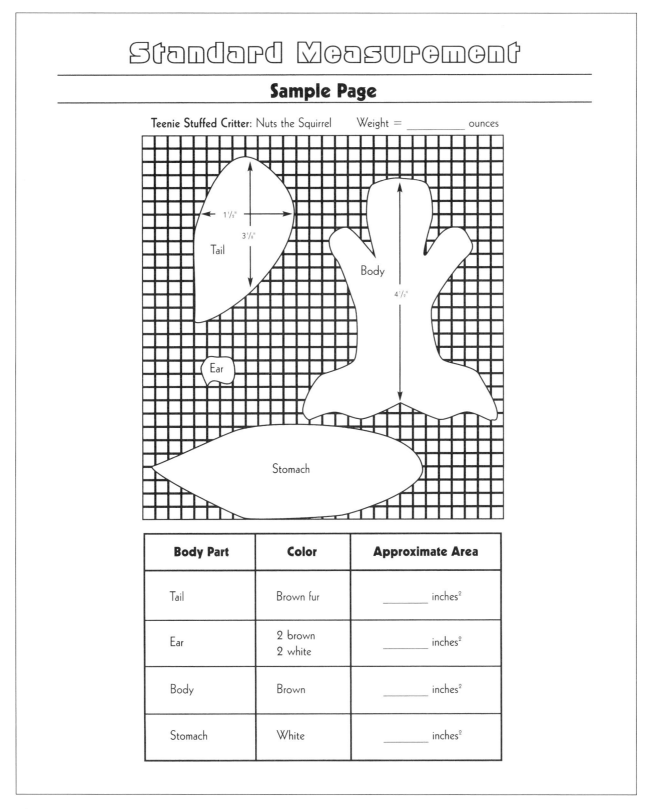

Body Part	Color	Approximate Area
Tail	Brown fur	_____ inches²
Ear	2 brown 2 white	_____ inches²
Body	Brown	_____ inches²
Stomach	White	_____ inches²

Figure A1.13

Standard Measurement

Rubric

Highlight the descriptor for each criteria that best fits the product. Add points earned to determine total rubric score.

	1 point	**2 points**	**3 points**	**4 points**
Body Parts Drawing	1 or more parts missing	Parts present, drawn inaccurately	Parts drawn accurately	Parts drawn accurately and neatly
Labeling	1 or more labels missing	Labels present, 1 or more spelled inaccurately	Labels present, spelled accurately	Labels present, spelled accurately, neat
Measurements	3 or more missing or inaccurate	1–2 missing or inaccurate	All present and accurate	All present, accurate, and neat
Area	1 or more missing or inaccurate	Not applicable	All present and accurate	All present, accurate and neat
Weight	Missing or inaccurate	Not applicable	Present and accurate	Present, accurate, and neat
Chart	1 or more categories missing	All categories present	Present and accurate	Present, accurate, and constructed with ruler or computer
Explanation	Missing or confusing	Ideas could be stated more clearly	Clearly stated	Clearly stated and easy to understand

Student name:_____   Evaluator:_____

Points possible = 28   Points earned = _____

Figure A1.14

Project 4 Overview

Unit Pricing

Standards: Decimal Operations, Communication, Problem Solving

Mathematics concepts: Unit pricing

Grade levels: 4 through 9

Materials: Grocery items

Task: Mrs. Jones just moved into your neighborhood and wants your input with her grocery shopping. She is trying to decide which product size is generally the best buy. She wants your help.

Suggested Student Procedures

1. Choose the largest and smallest size of any 10 items in a grocery store. (*Note:* If it is not possible for you to go to the grocery store, your teacher will bring two sizes of 10 items into the classroom.)

2. Record the name of each item, the size or quantity of each item, and the price of each item.

Example:	Hot Dogs	12 ounces	$0.78
		16 ounces	$1.04

3. Determine the unit price of each item and indicate which size is the better buy. (To find the unit price, divide the price by the number of ounces and round to the nearest cent.)

4. Complete the Reflections page.

Teacher Resources

Data Collection Chart (Figure A1.16)

Rubric (Figure A1.17)

Reflections page (Figure A1.18)

Figure A1.15

Unit Pricing

Data Collection Chart

Item Name	Size #1	Price #1	Unit Price #1	Size #2	Price #2	Unit Price #2	Better Buy
1.							
2.							
3.							
4.							
5.							
6.							
7.							
8.							
9.							
10.							

Figure A1.16

Unit Pricing

Rubric

Highlight each square that best describes the performance.

	0	1	2	3
Unit Pricing Item 1	Both missing or inaccurate	1 missing or inaccurate	Both accurate	Both accurate and rounded to the nearest cent
Item 2	Both missing or inaccurate	1 missing or inaccurate	Both accurate	Both accurate and rounded to the nearest cent
Item 3	Both missing or inaccurate	1 missing or inaccurate	Both accurate	Both accurate and rounded to the nearest cent
Item 4	Both missing or inaccurate	1 missing or inaccurate	Both accurate	Both accurate and rounded to the nearest cent
Item 5	Both missing or inaccurate	1 missing or inaccurate	Both accurate	Both accurate and rounded to the nearest cent
Item 6	Both missing or inaccurate	1 missing or inaccurate	Both accurate	Both accurate and rounded to the nearest cent
Item 7	Both missing or inaccurate	1 missing or inaccurate	Both accurate	Both accurate and rounded to the nearest cent
Item 8	Both missing or inaccurate	1 missing or inaccurate	Both accurate	Both accurate and rounded to the nearest cent
Item 9	Both missing or inaccurate	1 missing or inaccurate	Both accurate	Both accurate and rounded to the nearest cent
Item 10	Both missing or inaccurate	1 missing or inaccurate	Both accurate	Both accurate and rounded to the nearest cent
Better Buys	3 or more errors	2 errors	1 error	All accurate
Spelling	3 or more errors	2 errors	1 error	All accurate
Neatness	Difficult to read	Can be read with careful concentration	Neat	Perfect letters and numbers
Reflections	Difficult to understand	Lack clarity	Easy to understand	Easy to understand, show deep understanding of unit pricing

Student name: _____   Evaluator: _____   Points possible = 56   Points earned: _____

Figure A1.17

Unit Pricing

Reflections

Name _____

After compiling your data, what conclusions can you draw? Support your statements with examples.

Reflections:

Figure A1.18

Project 5 Overview

Complementary and Supplementary Angles

Standards: Geometry, Communication, Problem Solving

Mathematics concepts: Understanding and creating complementary and supplementary angles

Grade levels: 6 through 10

Materials: Examples of complementary and supplementary angles, protractors, scissors, glue, assorted colored paper

Purpose

1. To give students experience measuring angles using a protractor.

2. To give students experience finding and creating complementary and supplementary angles.

Suggested Student Procedures

1. On the paper provided, explain the meaning of complementary and supplementary angles.

2. Determine four pairs each of complementary and supplementary angles.

   Example: $42° + 48° = 90°$

   $115° + 65° = 180°$

3. Using a protractor and a separate piece of colored paper, draw each angle and label it with the appropriate number of degrees. Cut out each angle. Keep each angle with its pair.

   Example:

4. Fit the angle pairs onto the Supplementary Angles or Complementary Angles work page provided to show that they actually are complementary or supplementary angles. The fit should be exact. If it is not, make sure the angle size is correct and that it was cut carefully.

   Example:

Teacher Resources

Complementary and Supplementary Angles work pages (Figures A1.20, A1.21)

Rubric (Figure A1.22)

Figure A1.19

Complementary and Supplementary Angles

Supplementary Angles

Description: _____

_____

_____

_____ + _____ = 180°

_____ + _____ = 180°

Figure A1.20

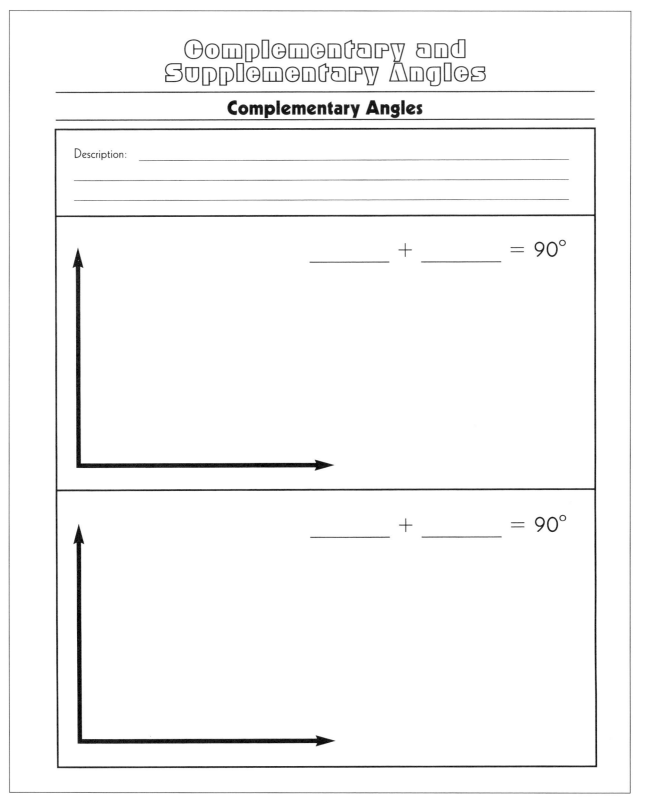

Complementary and Supplementary Angles

Complementary Angles

Description: _____

_____

_____

_____ + _____ = 90°

_____ + _____ = 90°

Figure A1.21

Complementary and Supplementary Angles

Complementary and Supplementary Angles Rubric

Circle the point value of the description that best applies to the finished product.

Complementary Angles Description	Description accurate and understandable. Example of concept included with definition. Spelling is perfect. Words are neatly written.	4
	Description accurate and understandable. Spelling is perfect. Words are neatly written.	3
	Description may be accurate but is difficult to understand OR spelling may be inaccurate OR neatness needs improvement.	2
	Description is difficult to understand, some spelling inaccuracies.	1
Pairs of Angles	Four angle pairs, neatly and accurately labeled each with sums of 90°	4
	Four angle pairs, accurately labeled each with sums of 90°	3
	Four angle pairs, accurately labeled	2
	Four angle pairs	1
Angle Measurement and Placement	Four angle pairs, drawn accurately and neatly glued to work pages showing that they are complementary	4
	Four angle pairs, drawn accurately and glued to work pages showing that they are complemenary	3
	Four angle pairs, drawn accurately and glued to work pages	2
	Four angle pairs glued to work pages	1
Supplementary Angles Description	Description accurate and understandable. Example of concept included with definition. Spelling is perfect. Words are neatly written.	4
	Description accurate and understandable. Spelling is perfect. Words are neatly written.	3
	Description may be accurate but is difficult to understand OR spelling may be inaccurate OR neatness needs improvement.	2
	Description is difficult to understand, some spelling inaccuracies.	1
Pairs of Angles	Four angle pairs, neatly and accurately labeled each with sums of 180°	4
	Four angle pairs, accurately labeled each with sums of 180°	3
	Four angle pairs, accurately labeled	2
	Four angle pairs	1
Angle Measurement and Placement	Four angle pairs, drawn accurately and neatly glued to work pages showing that they are supplementary	4
	Four angle pairs, drawn accurately and glued to work pages showing that they are supplementary	3
	Four angle pairs, drawn accurately and glued to work pages	2
	Four angle pairs glued to work pages	1

Student name:_____ Evaluator:_____ Points possible = 24 Points earned = _____

Figure A1.22

Appendix 2

Turning a 4-Point Rubric
Score Into a Letter Grade

When using a 4-point rubric, like the one in Figure A2.1, a score of 3 shows students are achieving at an acceptable level. After all, it is the second highest point value on the rubric. However, teachers who need to use letter grades are in a bind when grading this way. Often, the easiest way to grade is to take the score earned on the rubric and turn it into a percent. Mathematically, this is accomplished by dividing the points earned by the number of points possible. But this method alone will not give an accurate picture of student achievement. When earning 3 points on a 4-point rubric, a student has performed well. Three out of 4 points mathematically, however, is only a score of 75%. In many grading systems, the student is now left with an undeserved C or D letter grade.

Out of fairness to the students, and to calculate a more accurate reflection of student performance, the numbers can be manipulated slightly to achieve a grade that is more indicative of the quality of the product.

In the rubric shown in Figure A2.1, the student would receive an 83% as a result of the rubric score if the evaluator changed the rubric score into a percent. If that is the desired method, the evaluator could try using one of the options shown in Figures A2.2, A2.3, and A2.4 to determine the letter grade. These options might provide a fairer picture of achievement.

Figure A2.3 shows another option that can be used when assigning a grade to a point value.

A third option is demonstrated in Figure A2.4.

Each of these options aims to change a 4-point rubric scale into a 5-point letter grade scale. Using any of the three options provided should give teachers a more realistic picture of student achievement.

Name _____   Date _____

Solving Equations Grading Rubric				
Criteria	**1**	**2**	**3**	**4**
Equation solution	Answer only is shown	Initial equation and answer only are shown	Initial equation, steps, and answers shown	Initial equation, all steps, and answer are shown
Equation answer	Answer is incorrect	Steps are incorrect or not present, but answer is correct.	Steps are correct, but answer is incorrect	Steps are correct and answer is correct
Explanation of solution	Explanation is present, but demonstrates a lack of understanding	Explanation indicates a minimal understanding of procedure	Explanation indicates procedures are understood	Explanation clearly indicates procedures are understood at an advanced level

Points possible = 12
Points earned = 10

Figure A2.1

Option One

Turn the rubric score into a percent by dividing the points earned by the points possible, then use the scale provided.

Example:

Student earns 10 out of 12 points. $10 \div 12 = 83\%$ $83\% = B$

88–100 = A
75–87 = B
62–74 = C
50–61 = D
0–50 = F

This is a suggested point scale that seems to work fairly well. Percents can be adjusted up or down to best meet the needs of students.

Figure A2.2

Option Two

Determine the total points possible for the rubric. Divide the total possible by 5 to determine the increments for each point group. This is done because there are 5 grades in the A, B, C, D, F grading scale.

Example: rubric points possible total = 12   12/5 = 2.4

The (quotient) answer determines the highest point value for the F group.

F = 0 to 2.4 points

To determine the highest value for the D group, add the quotient to the highest point value in the F group.

D = 2.41 to 4.8 points

To determine the highest value for the C group, add the quotient to the highest point value in the D group.

C = 4.81 to 7.2 points

To determine the highest value for the B group, add the quotient to the highest point value in the C group.

B = 7.21 to 9.6 points

To determine the highest value for the A group, add the quotient to the highest point value in the B group.

A = 9.61 to 12 points

Figure A2.3

Option Three

Determine the points earned and divide by the number of criteria scored in the rubric. The answer will be a number between 1 and 4 when the rubric has a 1 to 4 point scale.

Example: On a 4-point rubric with 3 criteria, a student scores 10 points.

10 ÷ 3 = 3.33   3.33 = B

1–4 Rubric Scale	**1–4 Rubric Scale**	**0–3 Rubric Scale**
with no 0 used	with optional use of 0 for no evidence of a performance	A = 2.41 to 3.0
A = 3.41 to 4.0		B = 1.81 to 2.4
B = 2.81 to 3.4	A = 3.21 to 4.0	C = 1.21 to 1.8
C = 2.21 to 2.8	B = 2.41 to 3.2	D = 0.61 to 1.2
D = 1.61 to 2.2	C = 1.61 to 2.4	F = 0.0 to 0.6
F = 1.0 to 1.6	D = 0.81 to 1.6	
	F = 0.0 to 0.8	

Figure A2.4

Bibliography

Ainsworth, L., & Christinson, J. (1998). *Student generated rubrics.* Orangeburg, NY: Dale Seymour.

Allen, P. (1996, May). *Educational issues series: Performance assessment.* Madison: Wisconsin Education Association Council.

American Association of School Administrators. (2004). *Using data to improve schools.* Arlington, VA: KSA-Plus Communications.

Battista, M. (1999, February). The mathematical miseducation of America's youth. *Phi Delta Kappan,* pp. 425-433.

Bay, J., Reys, B., & Reys, R. (1999, March). The top 10 elements that must be in place to implement standards-based mathematics curricula. *Phi Delta Kappan,* pp. 503-506.

Bernhardt, V. (2005, February). Data tools for school improvement. *Educational Leadership,* pp. 66-69.

Bizar, M., & Daniels, H. (2005). *Teaching the best practice way.* Portland, ME: Stenhouse Publishers.

Black, P., & Wiliam, D. (1998). Inside the black box: Raising standards through classroom assessment. *Phi Delta Kappan Online.* Retrieved January 2001 from http://www.pdkintl.org/kappan/kbla9810.htm

Black, S. (1994, March). Doing the numbers. *Executive Educator,* pp. 41-44.

Bryant, D., & Driscoll, M. (1998). *Exploring classroom assessment in mathematics.* Reston, VA: National Council of Teachers of Mathematics.

Buehl, D. (1995). *Classroom strategies for interactive learning.* Schofield: Wisconsin State Reading Association Publications.

Burke, K. (1999). *How to assess authentic learning.* Thousand Oaks, CA: Corwin Press.

Burke, K. (2005). *How to assess authentic learning.* Thousand Oaks, CA: Corwin Press.

Burke, K. (2006). *From standards to rubrics in six steps.* Thousand Oaks, CA: Corwin Press.

Caudell, L. (1996, Fall). High stakes. *NW Education Magazine Online.* Retrieved October 1998 from http://www.nrel.org/nwedu/fall_96/article6.html

Cawelti, G. (2004). *Handbook of research on improving student achievement.* Arlington, VA: Educational Research Service.

Childs, R. (1989). *Constructing classroom achievement tests.* (ERIC Document Reproduction Service No. ED315426)

Costa, A., & Kallick, B. (1995). *Assessment in the learning organization.* Alexandria, VA: Association for Supervision and Curriculum Development.

Crosswhite, F. J., Dossey, J. A., & Frye, S. M. (1989). NCTM standards for school mathematics: Visions for implementation. *Mathematics Teacher, 82,* 664-671.

Danielson, C. (1997). *A collection of performance tasks and rubrics.* Larchmont, NY: Eye On Education.

Davison, M., Young, S., Davenport, E., Butterbaugh, D., & Davison, L. (2004, June). When do children fall behind? *Phi Delta Kappan,* pp. 752-761.

Depka. E. (2006). *Data guidebooks for teachers and leaders.* Thousand Oaks, CA: Corwin Press.

Dietel, R., Herman, J., & Knuth, R. (1991). *What does research say about assessment?* Oakbrook, IL: North Central Regional Educational Laboratory.

Eisner, E. (1999). The uses and limits of performance assessment. *Phi Delta Kappan Online.* Retrieved January 2001 from http://www.pdkintl.org/kappan/keis 9905.htm

Fitzpatrick, K. (1998). *Program evaluation: Mathematics.* Schaumburg, IL: National Study of School Evaluation.

Frye, S. (1989). The NCTM standards, challenges for all classrooms. *Arithmetic Teacher, 36,* 4-7.

Gardner, H. (1983). *Frames of mind: Theory of multiple intelligences.* New York: Basic Books.

Geocaris, C., & Ross, M. (1999, September). A test worth taking. *Educational Leadership,* pp. 29-33.

Glaser, R. (1998, September). *Reinventing assessment and accountability to help all children learn: Introductory remarks.* Paper presented at the annual conference of the National Center for Research on Evaluation, Standards, and Student Testing.

Guskey, T. (2005, November). Mapping the road to proficiency. *Educational Leadership,* pp. 32-43.

Hatfield, M., & Price, J. (1992). Promoting local change: Models for implementing NCTM's curriculum and evaluation standards. *Arithmetic Teacher, 39,* 34-37.

Jenkins, L. (1997). *Improving student learning.* Milwaukee, WI: ASQ Quality Press.

Jensen, E. (2005). Teaching with the brain in mind. Alexandria, VA: Association for Supervision and Curriculum Development.

Kaplan, A. (1998). *Math on call.* Wilmington, MA: Great Source Education Group.

Krueger, A., & Sutton, J. (2002). *EDThoughts: What we know about mathematics teaching and learning.* Aurora, CO: Mid-Continent Research for Education and Learning.

Kulm, G. (1999). Making sure that your mathematics curriculum meets standards. *Mathematics Teaching in Middle School, 4,* 536-541.

LaCoste, P. (1995). *Students grading students: Sharing responsibility for assessment.* Milwaukee: University of Wisconsin–Milwaukee.

Lazear, D. (1994). *Seven pathways of learning.* Tucson, AZ: Zephyr Press.

Mabry, L. (1999). Writing to the rubric: Lingering effects of traditional standardized testing on direct writing assessment. *Phi Delta Kappan Online.* Retrieved May 1999 from http:pdkintl.org/kappan/kmab9905.htm

Martin, H. (1998). *Integrating mathematics across the curriculum.* Thousand Oaks, CA: Corwin Press.

Martinez, M. (2006, May). What is metacognition? *Phi Delta Kappan,* pp. 696-699.

Marx, G. (2006). *Sixteen trends, their profound impact on our future.* Arlington, VA: Educational Research Service.

Marzano, R., & Kendall, J. (1996). *Designing standards-based districts, schools and classrooms.* Alexandria, VA: Association for Supervision and Curriculum Development.

Marzano, R., & Pickering, D. (2005). *Building academic vocabulary teacher's manual.* Alexandria, VA: Association for Supervision and Curriculum Development.

Marzano, R., Pickering, D., & Pollock, J. (2001). *Classroom instruction that works.* Alexandria, VA: Association for Supervision and Curriculum Development.

McTighe, J., & O'Connor, K. (2005, November). Seven practices for effective learning. *Educational Leadership,* pp. 10-17.

McTighe, J., & Wiggins, G. (1999). *The understanding by design handbook.* Alexandria, VA: Association for Supervision and Curriculum Development.

Merriam-Webster. (1989). *The new Merriam-Webster dictionary.* Springfield, MA: Author.

Mullis, I., Dossey, J. A., Owen, E. H., & Phillips, G. W. (1993). *NAEP 1992 mathematics report card for the nation and the states.* Washington, DC: United States Department of Education, Office of Educational Research and Improvement.

Munk, D., & Bursick, W. (1997, December). Can grades be helpful and fair? *Educational Leadership,* pp. 44-47.

National Assessment of Educational Progress. (1998). *Mathematics report card for the nation and the states. The nation's report card.* Retrieved January 1998 from http://nces.ed.gov/nationsreportcard/96report/97488.html

National Assessment of Educational Progress. (2005). *Mathematics report card for the nation and the states. The nation's report card.* Retrieved May 2006 from http://nces.ed.gov/nationsreportcard/nrc/reading_math_2005/s0017.asp?printver=

National Council of Teachers of Mathematics. (2000). *Principles and standards for school mathematics.* Reston, VA: Author.

O'Brien, T. (1999, February). Parrot math. *Phi Delta Kappan,* pp. 434-438.

Page, D. (2006). 25 tools, technologies, and best practices. *The Journal, 33,* 42-46.

Petrides, L. (2006). Using data to support school reform. *The Journal, 33,* 38-41.

Protheroe, N., Shellard, E., & Turner, J. (2004). *Helping struggling learners in the elementary and middle grades.* Arlington, VA: Educational Research Service.

Reeves, D. (1998). *Making standards work.* Denver, CO: Center for Performance Assessment.

Reeves, D. (2004). *Accountability for learning.* Alexandria, VA: Association for Supervision and Curriculum Development.

Rogers, S., & Graham, S. (1997). *The high performance toolbox.* Evergreen, CO: Peak Learning Systems.

Ronis, D. (2007). *Brain compatible mathematics* (2nd ed.). Thousand Oaks, CA: Corwin Press.

Rose, M. (1999, March). Make room for rubrics. *Instructor,* pp. 30-31.

Schmoker, M. (1996). *Results.* Alexandria, VA: Association for Supervision and Curriculum Development.

Schmoker, M. (2006). *Results now.* Alexandria, VA: Association for Supervision and Curriculum Development.

Schurr, S., Thomason, J., & Thomason. M. (1996). *Teaching at the middle.* Toronto, Ontario: D.C. Heath.

Slavin, S. (1989). *All the math you'll ever need.* New York: Wiley.

Stiggins, R. (2005, December). From formative assessment to assessment for learning. *Phi Delta Kappan,* pp. 324-328.

Stiggins, R. (1995). *Sound performance assessments in the guidance context.* (ERIC Document Reproduction Service No. ED388889)

U.S. Department of Education. (1993). *Help your child improve in test-taking.* Washington, DC: Author.

U.S. Department of Education. (1996). *Improving America's schools: A newsletter on issues in school reform.* Washington, DC: Author.

Wiggins, G. (1992, May). Creating tests worth taking. *Educational Leadership Online.* Retrieved October 1998 from http://www.bbpages.psu.edu/bbpages_references/40001/ 400015437.html

Wilson, L. (2005). *What every teacher needs to know about assessment.* Larchmont, NY: Eye On Education

Wolfe, P., & Brandt, R. (1998, November). What do we know from brain research? *Educational Leadership,* pp. 8-13.

Zemelman, S., Daniels, H., & Hyde, A. (1993). *Best practices.* Portsmouth, NH: Heinemann.

Index

Note: In page references, (f) indicates figures.

CORWIN PRESS

The Corwin Press logo—a raven striding across an open book—represents the union of courage and learning. Corwin Press is committed to improving education for all learners by publishing books and other professional development resources for those serving the field of PreK–12 education. By providing practical, hands-on materials, Corwin Press continues to carry out the promise of its motto: **"Helping Educators Do Their Work Better."**